Exploring Colorado State Parks

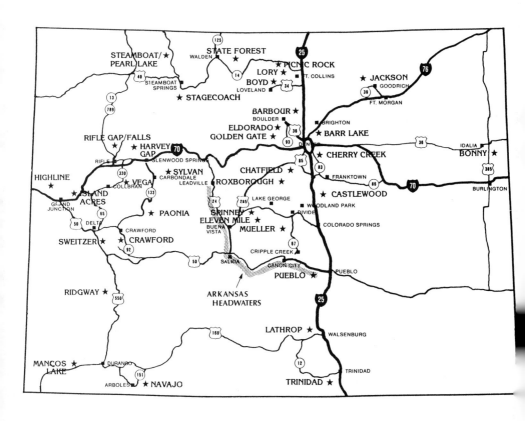

Exploring
Colorado State Parks

MARTIN G. KLEINSORGE

UNIVERSITY PRESS OF COLORADO

Copyright © 1992 by the University Press of Colorado
P.O. Box 849
Niwot, Colorado 80544

10 9 8 7 6 5 4 3 2 1

The University Press of Colorado is a cooperative publishing enterprise supported, in part, by Adams State College, Colorado State University, Fort Lewis College, Mesa State College, Metropolitan State College of Denver, University of Colorado, University of Northern Colorado, University of Southern Colorado, and Western State College.

Library of Congress Cataloging-in-Publication Data

Kleinsorge, Martin G., 1948–
    Exploring Colorado state parks / Martin G. Kleinsorge.
        p.   cm.
    Includes index.
    ISBN 0-87081-256-4 (cloth: alk. paper). — ISBN 0-87081-262-9
(pbk.: alk. paper)
      1. Colorado — Guidebooks. 2. Colorado — Pictorial works.
3. Parks — Colorado — Guidebooks. 4. Parks — Colorado —
Pictorial works. I. Title.
    F774.3.K54 1992
    917.8804'33 — dc20   92-9309
                                                  CIP

Contents

CONTENTS

Preface

Walking along the boardwalk at Barr Lake in the cool, crisp morning air, I witnessed the birth of a new day. As the burning sun peaked over the Great Plains, it cast a reddish glow over the snowcapped mountains of the Front Range. As I watched this colorful sight, I kept thinking about an article that I had read several years ago. I still don't remember who the author was or in what magazine the article appeared. I only remember a profound statement by the author that most Americans spend roughly 90 percent of their time indoors.

At first, I didn't believe this statement, but the more I thought about it, the more I realized it could be true. After all, most of the population live in urban areas and work indoors. We average an hour a day commuting to and from work. Our evenings are often dominated by the great human pacifier, the television set, and our weekends usually revolve around domestic and social activities, leaving little time for outdoor recreation.

I do feel, however, that times are changing. In our fast-paced, high-tech society, Americans, especially Coloradans, are realizing the value of outdoor recreation. People from all walks of life are yearning for mental and physical relaxation, the stimulation and rejuvenation of the human spirit that outdoor activities provide.

There are currently thirty-seven state parks, each with its own unique character and colorful history. Managed by the Colorado Division of Parks and Outdoor Recreation, these parks are scattered throughout the state, from the high plains to the snowcapped mountains to the desertlike plateaus of the Western Slope.

During the many months of writing and creating photographs for this book, my goal was to illustrate the personality of each state park and the recreational opportunities they offer.

Fishing, hiking, camping, biking, cross-country skiing, horseback riding, water sports, and nature study are only a few of the many one can participate in. From a wet and wild whitewater rafting trip down the mighty Arkansas River to tranquility in a mountainous setting, the state parks of Colorado have something for every member of the family.

Acknowledgments

A book of this magnitude requires the help and knowledge of many people. I am grateful to Tim King, marketing director for the Division of Parks and Outdoor Recreation, for his enthusiasm for the book and all the valuable information he provided throughout the year. I appreciate the information provided by Dave Kuntz, former program director of the Colorado Natural Areas, and Mike Carter of the Colorado Bird Observatory. I want to say thank you to Bill Perry, Jack Carrington, and Dick Sweitzer for sharing with me their knowledge of western Colorado history; to Bob and Dottie Pretti, John Boulton, and Martha Edwards of the Silt Historical Museum for helping me research the history of the Silt and Rifle areas; to Clarice Crowle for her knowledge of the Smokey Hill Trail; and to Peter Root for helping me find and identify the rare prairie moonwort.

A special thank you to all the park managers and park rangers who took the time from their busy schedules to answer all my questions; Steve Reese, Rose Bayless, Stew Pappenfort, Patricia Meador, Randy Rivers, Carol Leasure, Kevin Toby, Dave Uphoff, Doug Will, Bob Finch, Gary Buffington, Mike Widler, Carolyn Armstrong, Larry Kontour, Bob Toll, John Clark, Dave Spencer, Patricia Horan, Douglass Green, Richard Fletcher, Mike Severin, Larry Kramer, Craig Bergman, Gregg Nootbaar, John Weiss, Mike French, John Greerdes, Gene Rizzi, Jeff Riddle, Boyd Cornell, Dave Giger, Susie Trumble, Dan Overholser, Eugene Eiuhansen, Eric Harper, Dennis Scheiwe, Mike Taylor, Steve Werner, Russ Pallone, Brad Taylor, Butch Daniel, and Tim Metzger.

I am very grateful to Luther Wilson, Jody Berman, and the entire staff at the University Press of Colorado for their wisdom in seeing the value of this book and making it become reality.

Finally, for their constant support and inspiration, my gratitude and love goes to the two most important people in my life, my wife, Carol, and my daughter, Amanda.

Martin G. Kleinsorge

Exploring Colorado State Parks

A Historical Summary
of the Colorado Division of Parks
and Outdoor Recreation

Colorado's first state parks and recreation authority was created in 1937 when the state Board of Land Commissioners was given responsibility for state parks by the General Assembly. Unfortunately, the effort failed for lack of resources. The nation was rebounding from the Great Depression, and without adequate funding and staffing the project was doomed. Between 1950 and 1955, several attempts were made to establish a state parks and recreation department, but these also proved unsuccessful.

In 1957 Governor Stephen McNichols was authorized by the General Assembly to create the Colorado Parks and Recreation Department. Governor McNichols named Harold Lathrop director of the newly formed agency, a position he held until his death four years later. In 1959 McNichols signed a twenty-five year lease with the U.S. Army Corps of Engineers to make Cherry Creek Reservoir the first unit in the new state park system.

On June 31, 1960, the Parks and Recreation Department made its first purchase of land. A 200-acre tract in Gilpin County, designated "the ranch," became the nucleus of the now-10,000-acre Golden Gate Canyon State Park. Eleven Mile State Recreation Area also joined the park system under an agreement with the Denver Board of Water Commissioners. In August Sweitzer Lake was transferred to the state park system from the Game and Fish Department. After only three years in existence, the state park system had acquired 8,069 acres of land. A new duty was given to the department when it became responsible for the registration of boats. Temporary "boat wardens" under the supervision of a full-time "chief

1

warden" provided Colorado's first boat safety program. The growth and diversification of law enforcement reflected the broadening recreational pursuits of Colorado's population.

After the death of Harold W. Lathrop, George T. O'Malley was appointed the second director of the Parks and Recreation Department. On June 9, 1962, Lathrop State Park, named after Harold W. Lathrop, became the first unit designated as a state park (as opposed to a state recreation area). During 1962 the attendance at Colorado's state parks and recreation areas exceeded one million people.

The Parks and Recreation Department merged with the Game and Fish Department in 1963 to form the Game, Fish and Parks Department. George T. O'Malley was named assistant director in charge of parks.

In 1965 a user fee was established for designated parks and recreation areas. Naturally, the revenue was used to maintain the parks. During the following seven years, twenty-two new recreation areas were added to the Game, Fish and Parks Department.

In 1972 Senate Bill 42 separated the Game, Fish and Parks Department into the Division of Parks and Outdoor Recreation and the Division of Wildlife, both within the Department of Natural Resources. On August 14 a five-member citizen policy-making body was formed and given the authority to set rules and regulations for the parks. George T. O'Malley was named director of the Division of Parks and Outdoor Recreation.

As the park system grew, so did the number of visitors. The recreation facilities became so popular that park management had to be intensified. The division initiated its first campground reservation system in 1978. The previous year, it had been deemed necessary to staff a statewide boat, snowmobile, and off-highway vehicle patrol team. Park rangers began getting trained at law enforcement academies. The division developed its own basic law enforcement training center in 1978 and graduated nineteen park officers that year.

The early 1980s were a difficult time. Due to a dramatic drop in registered vehicles, the division ceased operation of the Off-Highway Vehicle Registration Program on December 31, 1981. The division faced a budget crisis, one that continued through 1982. Employees were required to take three days of leave without pay. However, there was a glimmer of hope: Colorado's new state lottery initiative was approved by the General Assembly, with the proceeds earmarked to benefit state and local parks. The new revenue slowly revitalized the park system.

Meanwhile, George T. O'Malley announced his retirement in 1982. In 1983, Ron Holliday was named the third director of Colorado's state park system.

In the late 1980s, Colorado was faced with a new problem. With Colorado's boating death rate being twice the national average, the General Assembly approved tough new boating laws in 1989. The legislature also approved a bill to reenact the Off-Highway Vehicle Registration Program in order to fund and maintain Colorado's diminishing motorized trails.

In January 1991 Ron Holliday resigned, and on May 13, 1991, Laurie Mathews was named director of the Division of Parks and Outdoor Recreation. In March, the decision was made to call all recreation areas in the system "state parks." This decision was made in an effort to avoid public confusion. (Previously, parks were reserved for land preservation, while recreation areas were reserved for outdoor activities on or near a body of water.) Although the names have been changed, the parks continue to be managed as in the past. On April 2 the division implemented a computerized, in-house camping reservation system.

The past decade has been a period of growth for the Division of Parks and Outdoor Recreation. There are thirty-seven state parks, and several new parks are planned to open in the near future. Future plans also include modernizing the older parks as the twenty-first century approaches.

Arkansas Headwaters Recreation Area

The Arkansas River begins its 1,400-mile journey to the Mississippi as a small mountain stream near the Continental Divide just below Fremont Pass. It soon develops into a lively river that passes below some of the loftiest peaks in the Rockies, including 14,433-foot Mount Elbert, the highest mountain in Colorado. The river drops 5,000 vertical feet during its first 125 miles, flowing through the Upper Arkansas Valley before carving through the granite walls of the Arkansas River canyon and the eight-mile-long Royal Gorge. The name Arkansas is derived from the Les Arkansas Indians, a tribe that lived along the river banks in an area now occupied by two states, Oklahoma and Arkansas. Historians believe that the first European to explore the area where the Arkansas leaves the mountains and enters the Great Plains was the Spanish explorer Juan de Ulibarri in 1706. Ulibarri witnessed the spring runoff, which often makes the muddy water of the Arkansas appear reddish in color, and named the river *Napestle*, an Indian word meaning "red water." The first American explorer, Zebulon Pike, followed the river as far as the Upper Arkansas Valley in 1806. In the coming years, this route led the way for hundreds of fur trappers.

In 1859, on a small tributary of the Arkansas near present-day Leadville, a prospector panned for a small amount of gold. Delirious with joy, he claimed that "this was California." The narrow valley, which became known as California Gulch, expanded the Colorado gold rush from the Front Range, and fortune hunters migrated to the new mining camp, called Ore City. The riches of California Gulch lasted only a few short years, but in 1878 large amounts of silver were discovered in the lead carbonate sand that previous miners had disregarded, and the mining industry thrived once again. The population of Ore City and

4

adjacent Leadville jumped from a few hundred people to just under 30,000.

As the silver mining industry grew, a new, more reliable means of transportation had to be developed. Bringing supplies into Leadville and carrying the precious metal over the Mosquito Mountains by wagon was slow and often dangerous. The most logical solution was to build a railroad up the natural corridor formed by the Arkansas River. Two railroad companies, the Denver and Rio Grande and the Atchison, Topeka and Santa Fe began laying track up the river. Just west of present-day Cañon City, they reached the 1,000-foot-high walls of Royal Gorge. At the entrance to the narrow chasm, they discovered that only one set of tracks could squeeze through the nearly vertical walls. Both railroads wanted the right-of-way through the gorge. As tension grew, workers from the competing companies began sabotaging each other's work; one crew would lay down a set of tracks, and the other company's crew would tear them up. There were numerous brawls, and on several occasions shots were fired. Surprisingly, there were no casualties.

Ultimately, the conflict had to be settled in court. The U.S. Circuit Court in Denver ruled that the Atchison, Topeka and Santa Fe Railroad should have the right-of-way through the canyon. The Denver and Rio Grande appealed the case to the U.S. Supreme Court, where it won a favorable judgment in March 1879. The Rio Grande got the right-of-way, but it would have to compensate the Santa Fe line for the construction work it had completed. Unfortunately, neither railroad could agree on a fair rate of compensation, which led to another court battle.

After many bitter arguments, the U.S. Circuit Court awarded the Santa Fe Railroad $1.4 million and ended the rivalry. The Denver and Rio Grande made the payments as laborers hastily resumed construction along the river. At that time, laborers were paid between $1.50 and $1.75 a day, and the company subtracted $3.50 per week for room and board, leaving the worker approximately $3.50 for six days of construction work. In July 1880, the Denver and Rio Grande Railroad finally reached the mining town of Leadville.

For the remainder of the century, the Upper Arkansas Valley experienced a succession of booms and busts. When the mining industry finally died out, the region turned to agriculture for its economic base. With an average of 300 sunny days a year and a mild climate, the area between Salida and Granite was ideal for cattle ranching and farming. It was also ideal for vacationing. Over a period of years, the Arkansas River became a favorite destination for recreationists throughout the state.

In a cooperative effort by the U.S. Bureau of Land Management and the Colorado Division of Parks and Outdoor Recreation, the Arkansas Headwaters Recreation Area has become one of the nation's most unusual recreation zones. The 148-mile-long park stretches along the Arkansas River from Granite, fifteen miles north of Buena Vista, to the western boundary of Lake Pueblo State Park. Developed in 1989, the Arkansas Headwaters Recreation Area provides unlimited opportunities for fishing, rafting, kayaking, hiking, camping, and sightseeing.

Whitewater rafting is the big attraction on the Arkansas River. In fact, there is more whitewater rafting on the Arkansas than on any other river in the United States. Within the recreation area, the river changes character several times, passing through varied geological features. There are over fifty-five rapids, with names like Wake Up, Maytag, River's Edge, Shark's Tooth, and Gosh Awful. Each rapid is classified according to the International Rating Scale:

I Easy: Small waves, no obstacles.

II Medium: Moderate waves with small drops, requires decent equipment.

III Difficult: Many high and irregular waves, narrow passages, requires expertise in maneuvering.

IV Very difficult: Large, irregular waves with fast water, hazardous rocks, and powerful eddies; precise maneuvering required, scouting mandatory for a first-time run, demands a very experienced and competent guide and excellent equipment.

V Extremely difficult: Very long, violent, and continuous rapid, powerful water with many dangerous obstacles; inspection of rapid absolutely necessary, requires the most proficient of operators and highest-quality equipment.

VI Ultimate limit of navigability: Loss of life possible; some consider such rapids unrunnable.

VII Has never been run successfully.

Numerous commercial outfitters offer rafting trips that range from "wet and wild" rides to family excursions for all ages. Float fishing trips are also available. (For a complete list of the different outfitters, call or write the chamber of commerce offices in Cañon City, Salida, or Buena Vista.) Private boaters are welcome to test their skill on the Arkansas. However, keeping in mind that the Arkansas is not a tame river, they should know their level of expertise, wear life jackets, and consult with others who have successfully boated there. All whitewater boats (rafts, kayaks, and canoes) must have the owner's name and address clearly written somewhere on the craft.

Fishing on the Arkansas can be a special experience. Anglers are challenged by the ten- to twelve-inch brown and rainbow trout that are common along the river. Fishing access areas are clearly marked, and fishing regulations may vary from one section of the river to another. Check with the Colorado Division of Wildlife for current regulations.

Arkansas Headwaters officially begins where the river's East Fork and Lake Fork meet. The stream is smooth, but quick-flowing until it reaches Pine Creek Canyon below Granite. As the Arkansas enters the canyon, it becomes a raging river, creating the Class V and VI Pine Creek Rapids. Leaving the canyon, it passes through a series of rapids called the Numbers, which extend down to the Railroad Bridge and challenge even the best kayakers and rafters. Although the land bordering the Numbers is privately owned, the Division of Parks and Outdoor Recreation has been negotiating with the owners to develop this area for recreational use.

Fourteen recreation sites along the river have been developed or are in the planning stages for future development. The Railroad Bridge Recreation Site, located about six miles north of Buena Vista, provides public river access for boating and fishing. There are no designated campsites, but the site is open to camping. The only facilities available are chemical toilets. Railroad Bridge can be reached by traveling north from Buena Vista on U.S. Highway 24 for nine miles. Turn east on Chaffee County Road 371 at the Otero Pump Station sign. Follow this road across the river, turn right, and drive south for three miles to Railroad Bridge. Chaffee County 371 follows the old railroad bed of the original Denver and Rio Grande Railroad parallel to the river.

The stretch of river between Railroad Bridge and Buena Vista, referred to as the Narrows, contains a long series of rapids rated as Class III and IV. As the river flows southward from the Pine Creek Canyon through Buena Vista, it runs along the east side of the valley. On the west side, the Collegiate Peaks — Oxford, Harvard, Yale, Columbia, and Princeton — protrude over 14,000 feet into the deep blue sky. A scenic

Arkansas Headwaters Recreation Area. The 14,197-foot Mount Princeton as seen from the scenic overlook just east of Johnson Village. From there, visitors have a beautiful view of the Upper Arkansas Valley and the Collegiate Peaks.

overlook with a spectacular view of the mountains and valley lies about a mile east of Johnson Village on U.S. Highway 24/285.

Approximately five miles south of Buena Vista on U.S. 285 is the turnoff to the Fisherman's Bridge and Ruby Mountain recreation sites. Turn east on Chaffee County Road 301 and drive a quarter of a mile to get to Fisherman's Bridge, a river access area for both fishing and boating. The only facilities available are chemical toilets. To reach Ruby Mountain, continue on Chaffee County 301 for another fourth of a mile, then turn east on Chaffee County 300 and follow it for two miles.

Ruby Mountain was named after the small bits of garnet, which look like tiny rubies, found in the rocks scattered across the hill. The recreation site, used for fishing and boating, has ten designated campsites, each with a table, grill, and toilet nearby. Water hydrants are not available.

Ruby Mountain is considered the northern gateway to Brown's Canyon, a scenic but challenging stretch of the river. As the river cuts through the canyon, it drops in elevation and builds up speed, creating crushing whitewater rapids, sharp turns, and narrow chutes. At the

8

southern portal of the canyon, the river passes Hecla Junction Recreation Site. Hecla Junction is a designated put-in/take-out area with dressing rooms and vault toilets available (for the convenience of rafters), several picnic sites, and eleven primitive campsites (each with a table and grill; water hydrants are not available). To reach Hecla Junction, follow Chaffee County Road 194 east from U.S. 285 for 2.5 miles.

As the river leaves the narrow Brown's Canyon, it reenters the open valley and makes a southeasterly turn known as Big Bend. Along Chaffee County 291, the Division of Parks and Outdoor Recreation has purchased thirty-five acres at Big Bend that it intends to develop into a river access area serving both boaters and anglers.

The headquarters for the Arkansas Headwaters Recreation Area is located just downstream from Big Bend in downtown Salida at 307 West Sackett Street. The headquarters building has a visitor center with displays that illustrate the river's history and geology. The center also provides the latest information on fishing and rafting conditions.

Beyond Salida, the river enters an area once referred to as the Upper Arkansas Canyon. In 1990 the state legislature changed the name to Bighorn Sheep Canyon at the urging of local residents. Stands of piñon and juniper trees dot the granite walls of this canyon, the site of the famous FIBArk (First in Boating on the Arkansas). Each June the town of Salida sponsors this premier river event, which began in 1949. It features several boat races, including a twenty-six-mile slalom race from Salida to Cotopaxi. Each race has two separate divisions, one for rafts and one for kayaks. There is also an event called the Hooligan race, where participants can ride on anything that floats — except a boat. Foot and bicycle races also take place during this four-day celebration.

Anglers appreciate this section of the river, as it slows into a series of still, deep pools flanked by rocky banks and gravel bars. The Division of Wildlife maintains public access areas along the river, as well as a fishing easement just downstream from Howard on the river's east bank. Just west of Howard is the Rincon Recreation Site, offering boating and fishing, several picnic sites, and primitive camping sites scattered along the river bank. The only facilities are tables, grills, and a chemical toilet. Vallie Bridge Recreation Site, roughly 1.5 miles northwest of Coaldale, also has river access for fishing and boating. The only facility available is a chemical toilet.

A few miles south of Vallie Bridge, the river turns to the northeast and enters the lower section of Big Horn Sheep Canyon. In this part of the canyon, often referred to as the "Grand Canyon of the Arkansas," the canyon walls are steeper, and the mighty river drops in elevation and picks up speed, creating numerous whitewater rapids. Visitors driving through this section of the canyon are intrigued by the bighorn sheep that come down from the high cliffs to drink from the river. The sheep have grown accustomed to people, cars, and trains. U.S. 50 is a busy road, so motorists should find a safe, secure parking area before viewing the wildlife.

Fishing is excellent along this stretch of the river. Groups of large rocks have been placed in the stream as part of a successful trout-habitat-improvement project. The rocks create large pools that serve as a resting area for fish fighting the strong currents.

Heading downstream on U.S. 50, one finds seven more recreation sites developed by the Division of Parks and Outdoor Recreation. The first, Lone Pine Recreation Site (located about a mile east of the KOA campground at Cotopaxi), is a river access area for fishing and boating. Facilities include several picnic tables with grills, and a chemical toilet nearby.

Continuing in an easterly direction, the next recreation site is Pinnacle Rock. Named after the unusual rock formation found at the west end of the parking area, Pinnacle Rock is a put-in/take-out area for rafters and kayakers. For their convenience, the site has dressing rooms and vault toilets; several picnic spots with tables and fire grills are also on hand.

The Five Points Recreation Site is a popular resting place for travelers on U.S. 50. Visitors can sit beneath the tall cottonwood trees at picnic tables and enjoy lunch while watching boaters battle the turbulent Five Points Rapid. Facilities include vault toilets that are handicapped accessible. A small primitive campground sits on the south side of U.S. 50, with nine sites suitable for tents, trailers, and pickup campers. The only amenities are tables and grills. Campers are advised to bring their own water.

Four recreation sites are grouped near the small village of Parkdale. The undeveloped Spikebuck and Bootlegger sites are small, unmarked pull-off areas that provide river access for fishing. The Parkdale Recreation Site is a major put-in/take-out point with a large parking lot, dressing rooms, vault toilets, picnic tables, and fire grills. From the junction of U.S. 50 and Fremont County Road 3, a short half-mile trail

Arkansas Headwaters Recreation Area. A wet and wild ride through the Five Points Rapid next to the Five Points Recreation Site along U.S. Highway 50.

leads to Parkdale South, another undeveloped recreation site providing river access for fishing and hiking.

As the river leaves the Parkdale area, it slices through the near-vertical walls of Royal Gorge. It took millions of years for the Arkansas River to carve through the hard rock of the Royal Gorge Plateau; many geologists believe that the course of the river was established before the plateau rose. During its eight-mile trek through the gorge, the river runs hard and fast. There are fourteen named rapids classified between Class III and V, giving rafters an exhilarating ride.

Each year thousands of people come to see the world's highest suspension bridge, which spans Royal Gorge. The bridge is a fourth of a mile long and stretches 1,055 feet above the river. Construction on the bridge began on June 5, 1929; it opened to the public on December 6, 1929. This nationally known landmark has attracted its share of daredevils. Pilots have flown small aircraft beneath the bridge, and parachutists have jumped from the span and plunged into the gorge.

As the Arkansas leaves the confines of the mountains and Royal Gorge and stretches across the Great Plains, it changes from a narrow,

Directions:
Between Granite and Salida, recreation sites can be reached via U.S. Highway 24 and 285. Between Salida and Cañon City, recreation sites can be reached via U.S. Highway 50.

Phone or write:
Arkansas Headwaters Recreation Area
Box 126
Salida, Colorado 81201
(719) 539-7289

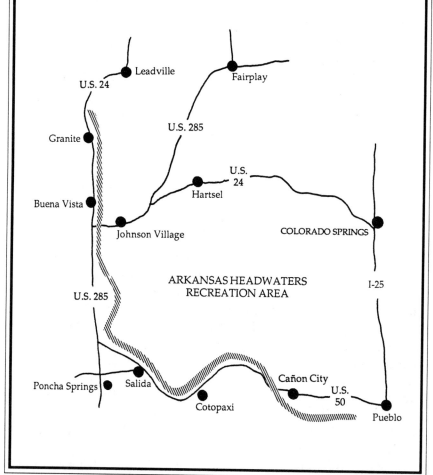

fast-flowing stream into a slow, meandering river. This section of the river is ideal for canoes and small rafts. However, several small dams and fallen trees could be hazardous to boaters.

The river is lined with cottonwood trees, willows, and a variety of flora that thrive on the prairie. This riparian zone is a natural habitat for a variety of wildlife. It's not unusual to see mule deer, coyotes, rabbits, and badgers along the river. Wild turkeys, eagles, hawks, great blue herons, and a variety of waterfowl also seek refuge along the densely wooded banks.

An annual or daily Colorado State Parks Pass is required to use the recreational facilities along the Arkansas River. Special day passes ($1.00 per person) and camping permits ($2.00 per campsite) can be purchased at self-service dispensers at each recreation site. Prices are subject to change.

Barbour Ponds State Park

It may seem unlikely that one could find outdoor recreation next to an interstate highway with thousands of cars whizzing by. However, Barbour Ponds State Park (formerly Barbour Ponds State Recreation Area) sits adjacent to Interstate 25 in the shadow of Longs Peak. A 130-acre preserve dedicated to families who don't want to drive a long distance to enjoy the great outdoors, the park is packed with people fishing, picnicking, and camping every summer weekend.

The park is named after Roy N. Barbour, a longtime Longmont resident and organizer of the Longmont Izaak Walton League. The ponds themselves did not exist until the late 1950s. Prior to that, the property was farmed by Albert and Edwin Anderson. The Andersons sold the land in 1958 to the Colorado Department of Highways, which used it to extract gravel for the construction of I-25. The excavation created four large water-filled pools. In 1962 the Colorado Game and Fish Department obtained the property by trading another segment of land to the Department of Highways. During the 1960s the area was slowly developed into a nature preserve.

Barbour Ponds has been administered by the Colorado Division of Parks and Outdoor Recreation since 1972. The lakes are fed by underground seepage from the St. Vrain River, which flows along the park's northern boundary. Unlike the water levels of other lakes that are filled this way, the levels of the Barbour Ponds are not dramatically affected by the changing seasons, because the St. Vrain has an unusually stable water flow. The river is fed with treated sewer water from the towns of Lyons and Longmont, and the additional input helps maintain the stream's volume during the drier fall and winter months. However, in 1969 the rain-swollen St. Vrain jumped its banks and flooded the area. During the cleanup, a wedge of land that divided two of the lakes was

Barbour Ponds State Park. The three lakes at Barbour Ponds provide anglers of all ages with some of the best warm-water fishing in northern Colorado.

Barbour Ponds State Park. By walking or driving around the lakes, the careful observer can observe and photograph a variety of migratory birds and wildlife.

removed. The final result was one large lake in the northern half of the park and two smaller ponds on the west and south sides.

These eighty acres of water provide anglers with some of the best warm-water fishing in northern Colorado. The lakes are stocked with trout, catfish, bass, bluegill, and crappie. There is no designated fishing area for handicapped visitors, although several areas along the shore of each lake are handicapped-accessible.

The ponds make a good destination for a daytime outing. Families can enjoy the shaded pondside picnic area or any of the sheltered picnic tables scattered around the lakes. Nature study and nature photography are also favorite activities at Barbour. Near the entrance station is the trailhead to the Muskrat Nature Trail, built by the Young Adult Conservation Corps in 1977. The trail offers a peaceful walk that extends one-fourth of a mile through a lakeside marsh. By walking along the trail or around any of the lakes, the careful observer can find a variety of resident and migratory birds and waterfowl, including the great blue heron. Park rangers will lead groups on interpretive nature walks through the park on request.

Barbour has sixty campsites located in two campgrounds. These

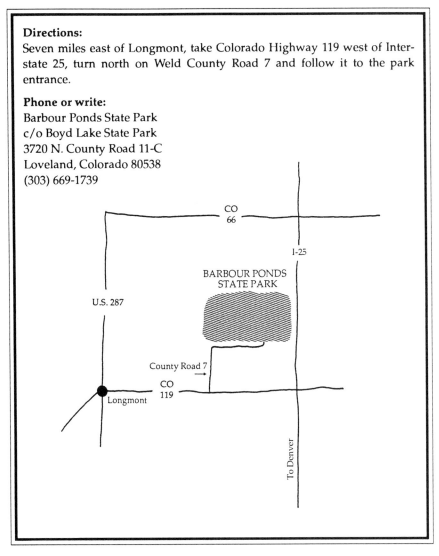

Directions:
Seven miles east of Longmont, take Colorado Highway 119 west of Interstate 25, turn north on Weld County Road 7 and follow it to the park entrance.

Phone or write:
Barbour Ponds State Park
c/o Boyd Lake State Park
3720 N. County Road 11-C
Loveland, Colorado 80538
(303) 669-1739

sites can accommodate tents, campers, trailers, and larger motor homes. Most of the sites at the East Campground are shaded by tall cottonwood trees and include a table and grill, with a vault toilet nearby. At the south end of the campground is a horseshoe pit built by Boy Scout Troop 601. The West Campground has sheltered tables and grills at each site. Additional facilities include vault toilets, water hydrants, and a playground. There are no electric hookups, although future plans include expanding the campgrounds with full facilities.

Barr Lake State Park

At dawn during the nesting season, Barr Lake State Park has the feel of a remote jungle. The songs, chirping, screeching, and quacking of thousands of birds is very intense.

Located approximately thirty miles northeast of downtown Denver, this 2,600-acre park has become a wildlife sanctuary. The lakeshore is lined with stands of cottonwood trees, marshes, and aquatic plant growth that provide food and shelter for waterfowl and nongame birds. Of the 440 species of birds recorded in Colorado, over 330 have been observed at Barr Lake; of these, 65 species nest there, and approximately 30 are listed as endangered, diminishing, or threatened. With a pair of binoculars or a spotting scope, naturalists can observe red-winged and yellow-headed blackbirds, pelicans, meadowlarks, owls, and western grebes, to name a few. Bird watchers enjoy the Barr Lake Heron Rookery, where great blue herons share a nesting area with egrets and cormorants.

Since the winter of 1986, Barr Lake has been the nesting site for a pair of bald eagles, making it one of less than ten known bald eagle nesting sites in Colorado. A student on a nature walk first spotted a pair of bald eagles on a nest in the heron rookery. Park rangers continued to observe the eagles as they apparently incubated an egg. Sadly, numerous spring storms raged through the area, causing the eagles to abandon the nest. The following year a pair of eagles repeated the ritual of nest building and courtship. During the incubation period the male disappeared, and after a few days the female abandoned the nest. A wildlife biologist retrieved an egg, which studies showed was about a week away from hatching.

Each year since, a pair of bald eagles has returned to the nest and produced offspring. Unfortunately, the birds are not banded, so there is no way to determine if they are the same eagles from year to year.

Barr Lake State Park. Since the winter of 1986, Barr Lake has been the nesting site for a pair of bald eagles. The site is unique in that it is one of less than ten known bald eagle nesting sites in Colorado.

However, for the past three years, the young chicks have been banded. In 1989 two young eagles fledged the nest; in 1990 two more fledged; and in 1991 there were three fledglings. Only 50 percent of the young eagles survive their first year. Although they quickly learn to fly, learning to survive can be a difficult challenge — after all, good hunters are made and not born.

The Colorado Bird Observatory was founded in 1988 with headquarters at Barr Lake. In cooperation with the Colorado Division of Parks and Outdoor Recreation and the Colorado Division of Wildlife, the observatory developed the Barr Lake Eagle Watch, a unique and valuable program in which volunteers monitor the daily behavior of the eagles. Observers go through a training session, then watch the eagles in four-hour shifts throughout the spring and summer. The information gathered by the eagle watchers is entered into a computer, analyzed, and used to answer questions about eagle behavior and habitat. (For more information about becoming an eagle watcher, call the Colorado Bird Observatory office.)

In addition to the many bird species found at Barr Lake, approximately twenty species of mammals can be seen and photographed. The careful observer can spot both mule deer and white-tailed deer, as well as red fox, cottontail rabbits, skunks, and an occasional coyote. Because of the development surrounding the park, many prairie animals are no longer found at Barr Lake. These include the pronghorn antelope, desert cottontail, white-tailed jackrabbit, and black-tailed prairie dog.

Another departed prairie species, the bison, played a part in the history of Barr Lake. In the early 1850s, the area now occupied by the lake was a large buffalo wallow. In an effort to control pesky insects, bison would gather at the depression and roll in the mud. As white people settled the area, the bison disappeared and the wallow came to be used as a holding area for cattle roundups. These cattle were included in the famous cattle drives on the Goodnight-Loving cattle trail that passed nearby on its way to Wyoming.

The Barr Lake area grew quickly during the 1880s. Construction of the Chicago, Burlington and Quincy Railroad began in Denver in 1881 and culminated on May 14, 1883. The last spike was driven in Platte Summit on the west side of the lake. Platte Summit was renamed Barr City on August 5, 1887, in honor of a civil engineer employed by the railroad.

Agriculture became the dominant industry around Barr City. Many farmers realized that the old buffalo wallow would make an ideal reservoir for irrigation. Thus, five enterprising men developed the Burlington Ditch, Reservoir and Land Company in 1884. By 1886 they had built the Burlington Ditch, which diverted water from the South Platte River at the Riverside Cemetery in Denver and transported it to newly formed Barr Lake.

Early maps of the area show that there were originally two lakes. The main lake was known as Lake Oasis or Oasis Reservoir. Barr Lake, which was fed by the Burlington Ditch, was a smaller lake to the south. The old ditch and its headgate are still visible at the south end of Barr Lake.

The combination of agriculture, water, and transportation spurred rapid development at Barr City. In 1887 the Barr City Land Company was formed to sell lots for commercial use. The town flourished with new businesses, a creamery, a brickyard, a Grange hall, a new church, and a new school. During the mid-1880s the area became popular with outdoor sportsmen. The October 18, 1895, edition of the *Brighton Register* called Lake Oasis a great shooting and fishing resort. The following year, the Oasis Outing Club was formed.

The Burlington Ditch, Reservoir and Land Company made plans to enlarge Oasis Reservoir in 1903. At the same time, the Denver Reservoir and Irrigation Company acquired the rights to the canal and reservoir, and the new company proceeded with the expansion of the dam. The two lakes were joined, and the enlarged Barr Lake was raised from 5,074 feet to 5,091 feet above sea level. Along with the new 7,000-foot-long dam, the Burlington-O'Brian Canal was built to supply water to the lake at a higher elevation. In 1909 the Denver Reservoir and Irrigation Company was reorganized as the Farmers Reservoir and Irrigation Company.

The 1930s were a troublesome time for Barr City. The railroad announced the closing of the Barr City station in 1931 because of the lack of business. One by one establishments began to close in the once-thriving community. Meanwhile, the City and County of Denver began operation of a sewage treatment plant that gave only primary treatment to wastewater before discharging it into the South Platte River. The discharge point was about a quarter of a mile upstream from Burlington-O'Brian Canal headgates, so most of the debris was diverted into the canal and deposited into Barr Lake. It was only a matter of time before the lake became a sludge-filled sewage lagoon.

21

Barr Lake State Park. The Barr Lake Wildlife Center is a great place to begin an adventure at Barr Lake. The Wildlife Center provides unique learning opportunities for children and adults. Visitors can get a close-up view of live turtles, lizards, and a bull snake. There are several display panels that illustrate the wildlife and plants common to the prairie.

From the early 1950s through 1965, hundreds of complaints were received by state and local health authorities about the condition of the lake. Barr Lake had become one of the most polluted bodies of water in Colorado. It not only created a health hazard for people, it also threatened wildlife and the quality of irrigation water. The lake's condition began improving in 1965 when Metropolitan Sewage District Number 1 was formed in Denver. The district built a new plant with complete treatment capabilities. Treated water from this new plant was discharged below the Burlington-O'Brian Canal headgates.

In 1973 the Colorado Division of Parks and Outdoor Recreation began purchasing land around Barr Lake. During the mid-1970s facilities were constructed to accommodate public access, and in April 1977 the new Barr Lake State Park opened.

Barr Lake is a day-use area with recreational facilities located on the east side of the lake. The southern half of the lake is a wildlife refuge, while the northern half is open to boating and fishing. Without a doubt,

Barr Lake State Park. From the boardwalk along the Niedrach Nature Trail, visitors can view a variety of birds and waterfowl. During the low-water season in late summer, numerous mammals, including mule deer and white-tailed deer, can be observed from the trail.

nature study is the big attraction. The Barr Lake Wildlife Center, operated by the Division of Wildlife, provides a unique learning opportunity for children — and adults. Several display panels illustrate the animals and plants common to the prairie. Visitors can get a close-up view of live turtles, lizards, and a bull snake. On request, park naturalists will lead anyone from preschoolers to senior citizens on interpretive nature walks.

Beginning at the wildlife refuge bridge, visitors can cross the Denver and Hudson Canal (a branch of the Burlington-O'Brian Canal) paralleling the eastern shoreline to the main trail, which ventures nine miles around the lake. The trail follows the old ditch-rider's road that has been in existence since the early 1900s; it is open to hiking, bicycling, (with thorn-proof tires), and horseback riding.

About twenty yards south of the bridge, a short trail leads to the right-of-way from the main trail. This is known as the Niedrach Nature Trail. Named after a Denver ornithologist who studied the birds at Barr Lake during the first half of this century, the trail passes along the shore

Directions:
From Denver, take Interstate 76 north to Bromley Lane. Go east to Picadilly Road and drive south to the park entrance.

Phone or write:
Barr Lake State Park
13401 Picadilly Road
Brighton, Colorado 80601
(303) 659-6005
Wildlife Center: (303) 659-1160
Colorado Bird Observatory: (303) 659-4348

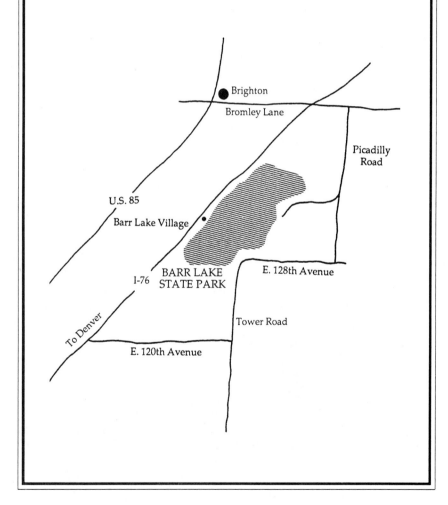

through an open field and across a boardwalk that extends over the lake. Another boardwalk lies about 1.5 miles southwest of the wildlife center. This boardwalk extends about 100 yards over the lake and ends at a gazebo, where there is a scenic view of the lake and the heron rookery.

A section of the main trail just north of Barr Lake Village (formerly Barr Lake City) follows the railroad tracks for about a quarter of a mile. The tracks are built on a dike that holds in the lake's water. This is an area of concern for hikers, especially during the high-water season. When trains pass by, it can prove to be a frightening experience, particularly for people on horseback.

At the northeast corner of the park, the trail winds past an old stone house. The structure was built in 1890 under the supervision of Emil Bruderlin, a prominent Denver businessman engaged in the book-binding trade. Designed to reflect the Bruderlins' Swiss heritage, the house was built from sandstone brought in by railroad from the Deckers area. Unfortunately, the Bruderlin family enjoyed its new home for only a short time. Emil Bruderlin was killed in an accident at Barr City in April 1892 attempting to jump back on a moving train to retrieve a package.

The trail continues below the dam. Along the east side of the lake, it extends southward between the lake and the Denver and Hudson Canal and passes by the north parking lot on its return to the wildlife center.

Barr Lake has thirty-four individual picnic sites, twelve of them with sheltered tables, in three separate locations. One picnic area is located next to the wildlife refuge bridge; the Cottonwood picnic area, with six tables shaded by mature cottonwood trees, is next to the main park road; and the third picnic area is next to the north parking lot at the northeast corner of the lake.

Boaters have access to the lake via a one-lane bridge that crosses over the Denver and Hudson Canal at the north parking lot. Only sailboats, canoes, sailboards, and boats with electric motors or gasoline motors under ten horsepower are permitted on the northern half of the reservoir. During the late summer months when the water level is low, boating activities may be limited.

Fishing is also popular at Barr Lake, especially bow fishing for carp during the spawning season. The Division of Wildlife periodically stocks the lake with catfish, crappie, large and smallmouth bass, bluegill, tiger muskie, perch, and rainbow trout.

Bonny State Park

Driving across the vast, semiarid plains, one can only imagine the hardships cast upon the early pioneers. After all, Major Stephen H. Long, on his expedition across the prairie in 1820, declared the land an "uninhabitable, forsaken land." Despite the scarcity of water and the presence of hostile Indians, the newcomers continued westward. They brought with them their cattle, sheep, agriculture, and barbed-wire fences. The combination of these elements brought an end to the openness of the Great Plains.

The pristine prairie, with its gently rolling hills, was formed by the forces of ice, wind, water, and fire — and, of course, the hand of modern man. Although most of these forces are no longer at work, each left a distinguishing mark on the prairie landscape and its unique ecosystem.

At least four times during the past two million years, great sheets of glacial ice more than a mile thick spread down from the Arctic to cover Canada and the northern third of the United States. The huge glaciers were powerful enough to grind vast amounts of rock into tiny mineral-rich particles. As the last of the glaciers receded northward between 10,000 and 15,000 years ago, a barren landscape vulnerable to erosion was exposed. Over the years, strong winds picked up the finely ground rock particles, carried them for hundreds of miles, and redeposited them in a thick layer over the Great Plains. As the soils were blown in from the north, rivers and streams emerged. Dunes were carved and rearranged by water, creating rolling hills and valleys.

This surface layer is known as *loess*, a German word meaning "wind-deposited silty soils." Loess soils are the foundation of the landscape in eastern Colorado, western Kansas, and Nebraska. Loess prairies fall in a transition zone between the tallgrass prairies to the east and shortgrass prairies to the west. Moisture is the key ingredient that determines what type of grass grows on the plains: Tallgrass prairies receive over twenty inches of rain annually, while shortgrass prairies receive less than twelve inches.

Fires were once common across the plains, with the prairie burning every few years. These fires were either caused by lightning or set by the Indians. The Native Americans understood the regenerative effects of fire on the prairie ecosystem. White settlers were frightened by the fires and tried to prevent them from spreading.

The settlers planted crops, breaking the sod that had tied the soil for thousands of years. Because of severe drought, during the 1870s and 1890s croplands were transformed into pastures for sheep and cattle. Unfortunately, the heavy grazing prevented native grasses such as little bluestem, sideoats grama, and buffalo grass from becoming reestablished. The farmers introduced foreign grasses such as smooth bromegrass and cheatgrass. As the new grasses began to thrive, the remaining native species were soon excluded. By the late 1920s, almost every acre of the original prairie ecosystem had been plowed and fenced. The strong, restless winds blew the turned soil across the arid plains as farmers became victims of the "black blizzards," swirling clouds of dirt. This was the beginning of the Dust Bowl years of the early 1930s.

In the spring of 1935, it rained constantly during the first two weeks of May, saturating the central plains. On May 31 two storm systems converged over eastern Colorado, western Kansas and Nebraska, producing twenty-four inches of rain in a forty-minute period. The resulting flood devastated area towns and farms causing widespread death and destruction.

In the wake of this disaster, the U.S. Bureau of Reclamation began searching for a site to build a reservoir for flood control and irrigation. The decision was made to use the South Republican State Wildlife Area near the confluence of the South Fork of the Republican River and Landsman Creek. Congress authorized construction of the Bonny Dam in 1946. Ground breaking did not take place until December 8, 1948, and the project was completed May 4, 1951.

Bonny Dam and Reservoir were named after the small town of Bonny, a short-lived settlement that served the area as rural post office from 1915 through 1924. Located about five miles southeast of today's reservoir, Bonny reached a population of 110 people. The town was named after Isaac Bonny, the postmaster and a leading citizen of the community.

Bonny State Park (formerly Bonny State Recreation Area) became part of the state park system in 1963. Today, the 7,000-acre preserve is jointly administered by the Colorado Division of Wildlife, which has jurisdiction over fish and wildlife resources, and the Division of Parks and Outdoor Recreation. Camping, water sports, and fishing are the big attractions at Bonny. Recreational facilities are found along the north and south shores.

Bonny State Park has four campgrounds with a total of 200 camp-sites. Each campground can accommodate tents, trailers, pickup camp-ers, and motor homes. On the south side of the lake is the large, grassy Wagon Wheel Campground. The sites here are equipped with tables and grills. Some of the tables are artificially sheltered, while others are shaded by tall cottonwood trees. Additional facilities include flush and vault toilets, showers, a laundry, water hydrants, a volleyball field, and a children's playground. A dump station is located at the campground entrance.

The East Beach Campground is located at the southeast corner of the lake. A section of the campground is reserved for tents only; tables and fire rings are provided at each site, with vault toilets and water hydrants nearby. At the northeast corner of the lake is the North Cove Campground, which has a group campsite along with numerous indi-vidual campsites. Some are sheltered, while others are shaded by tall trees; each site is equipped with a table and grill, with vault toilets and water hydrants nearby. A boat ramp is also available. Finally, the Foster Grove Campground, in the northwest section of the park, has campsites nestled beneath tall cottonwood trees. Tables and grills are provided at each site. Both flush and vault toilets are available, along with showers, water hydrants, a children's playground, and a dump station.

The Bonny Dam Marina, located next to the Wagon Wheel Camp-ground, has two boat ramps, along with boat and slip rental, fuel, and a fish-cleaning station. The marina concession building stocks food, bev-erages, ice, and fishing and camping accessories.

Those who prefer swimming to boating can take advantage of two swimming areas at Bonny. A small, shallow area is located below the marina store, only a short walk from the Wagon Wheel Campground. At the larger and deeper West Beach swimming area, west of the marina, no lifeguards are on duty, so individuals swim at their own risk.

Waterskiing, jet skiing, sailing, and windsurfing are other popular water sports at Bonny. The East Ski Beach, located next to the East Beach

Bonny State Park. The rolling hills of the open prairie are home to over 250 species of plants and grasses.

Campground, is a designated take-off/drop-off area for water-skiers. Skiers also use an area adjacent to the West beach.

A day-use facility with numerous picnic sites sits next to the marina and stretches along the south shoreline. There is a large pavilion that can accommodate groups of up to 100 people. The pavilion can be reserved in advance and provides water, electricity, and a variety of cooking amenities. Several additional picnic areas dot the north shoreline, including one at Pikes Point.

Bonny has developed a reputation as one of Colorado's finest warm-water fisheries. Anglers are delighted with the thriving populations of walleye, northern pike, large and smallmouth bass, crappie, bluegill, catfish, and wipers.

Aside from being a popular recreation area, Bonny is one of the few remaining areas in Colorado where people can find true loess soil. The park has approximately eighty acres of loess prairie located in three different sites, including the twenty-acre Bonny Prairie Natural Area in the northeast corner of the park. Designated a Colorado Natural Area in 1988, the site has over 250 species of plants and grasses and a short trail

Bonny State Park. The prairie moonwort is a tiny, inconspicuous fern that grows in sandy soil. It has a growing season of about six weeks. The fern in this photo is an immature plant, about three weeks old.

with thirteen interpretive stations that illustrate the history, geography, vegetation, and wildlife of the region.

In the spring of 1990, naturalist Peter Root, park manager Dave Uphoff, and Colorado Natural Areas director Dave Kuntz discovered the prairie moonwort, a tiny, inconspicuous fern that grows in sandy soil. In over eighty acres of loess prairie, they found only three of the delicate plants, each less than two inches tall. With a growing period of about six weeks, this species is extremely rare on the Great Plains.

After studying the rolling sand hills, many visitors lift their eyes skyward and are surprised to see turkey vultures riding the thermals overhead. The diversity of habitats on the open prairie ecosystem provides food and shelter to numerous birds. Bonny lies in a natural flyway and is a resting place for more than 250 species of birds and waterfowl during the migrating season. Some 30,000 to 50,000 birds winter in the area. Throughout the year the careful observer can find and photograph pelicans, osprey, eagles, and prairie falcons. A variety of smaller birds populate the densely wooded shoreline and the riparian zone along the west side of the park, along with mule and white-tailed deer, wild

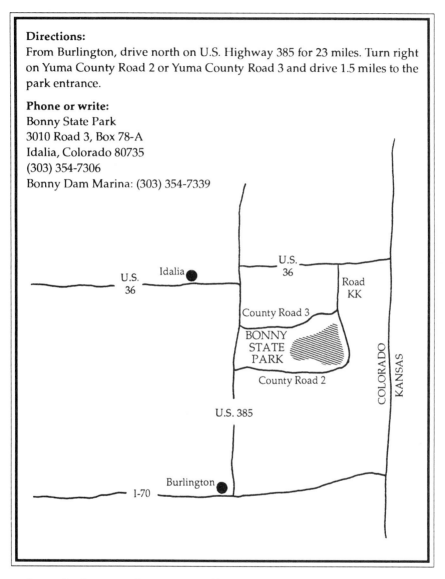

Directions:
From Burlington, drive north on U.S. Highway 385 for 23 miles. Turn right on Yuma County Road 2 or Yuma County Road 3 and drive 1.5 miles to the park entrance.

Phone or write:
Bonny State Park
3010 Road 3, Box 78-A
Idalia, Colorado 80735
(303) 354-7306
Bonny Dam Marina: (303) 354-7339

turkeys, badgers, and coyotes. Bull snakes and prairie rattlesnakes also live in the park. Although these snakes generally shy away from people, they will strike if provoked.

Hunting of waterfowl and big and small game is legal in designated areas during the regular hunting season. Dates and regulations change annually. For detailed information on each season, call or write the Division of Wildlife.

Boyd Lake State Park

A mile east of Loveland, surrounded by farmland and residential areas, stands an oasis on the prairie, a place to relax and have fun on the high plains while admiring the grandeur of the Rockies. Boyd Lake State Park (formerly Boyd Lake State Recreation Area) is becoming a water sports haven for northern Colorado, attracting families who enjoy camping and picnicking as well as water sports.

Boyd Lake began as a state fishing area in 1958 and was designated a state recreation area in 1965. At that time the park was underdeveloped, with only a few primitive facilities. The lake was nearly abandoned as a state recreation area in 1978. The government's lease with the Greeley-Loveland Irrigation Company (which owned the lake) was about to expire, and the state was reluctant to continue operating a second-rate site. However, the citizens of Loveland, outraged at the thought of losing Boyd Lake, encouraged the state legislature to purchase the recreation rights along with 196 acres of land. Thus began the transformation of Boyd Lake. With funds received from the Colorado Lottery, the Colorado Division of Parks and Outdoor Recreation decided to upgrade Boyd Lake and use it as a model to demonstrate how parks could be improved with additional revenue.

Since 1981 more than $4 million has been spent on the park. The money was used to install water and sewer pipes, electricity, and telephone services. The facilities are taken for granted by newcomers to the area, but to old-timers they represent major progress. The park is now one of the most modern in the state park system.

Boyd Lake was originally designed and is still used for irrigation and municipal water storage for the Loveland-Greeley area. It gets its water from Grand Lake, on the west side of the Continental Divide, as part of the Colorado–Big Thompson Project approved by Congress in

Boyd Lake State Park. Boyd Lake gets its water from Grand Lake on the west side of the Continental Divide. The lake averages between 1,700 and 1,800 acres of water and provides some of the best warm-water fishing and water sports in northern Colorado.

1937. Water from the Colorado River and surrounding streams is gathered in Lake Granby, pumped uphill into a canal, and channeled into Shadow Mountain Lake and then into Grand Lake. From there water flows into the Alva B. Adams Tunnel and travels 3,780 feet below the Continental Divide to Marys Lake, then by tunnel to Lake Estes near Estes Park. The water is then diverted down the Big Thompson River to a series of tunnels and irrigation canals that fill several Front Range reservoirs, including Boyd Lake.

Depending on the season and the amount of water used for irrigation, the park averages between 1,700 and 1,800 acres of water and 196 acres of land along the west shore. The rest of the lake is bordered by private property. The lake is a prime fishing area in northern Colorado. The Colorado Division of Wildlife periodically stocks it with trout, walleye, bass, catfish, and crappie.

Boyd Lake features a marina that can accommodate both power boats and sailboats. Two boat ramps serve the lake. The ramp at the marina in the southern half of the lake serves power boats used for waterskiing and fishing. The marina provides a concession for boat rentals, fuel, and boating and fishing supplies. The second ramp, north of the marina along the northwest shore, is used primarily for sailboats, which dominate the northern half of the lake. Sailboard rentals and lessons are also available.

Swimmers and sunbathers enjoy the combination swim beach and day-use area, located in a cove with 1.5 acres of sand. Nearby, a pavilion surrounded by three acres of manicured lawns houses a modern, solar-heated bathhouse with locker rooms and showers, as well as a first-aid station. There are sixty picnic sites in this area, and a store that offers food and drinks. Other attractions are the volleyball court and two separate playgrounds for children.

At Mariner Point, located on a peninsula just north of the marina, a large group picnic area can accommodate gatherings of up to 200 people. From this point, a scenic view of the lake and the marina can be had. This area has horseshoe pits, a volleyball court, a children's playground, and ample room for organized games.

Boyd Lake's campground has 148 pull-through sites that can harbor anything from tents to the largest of motor homes. This modern campground provides a table and grill at each site, flush toilets, showers, and a playground.

Directions:
Take U.S. Highway 34 west from Interstate 25, to Madison Avenue in Loveland. Turn north and drive 1.5 miles. Turn right on Larimer County Road 24E and follow to the park entrance.

Phone or write:
Boyd Lake State Park
3720 N. County Road 11C
Loveland, Colorado 80538
(303) 669-1739

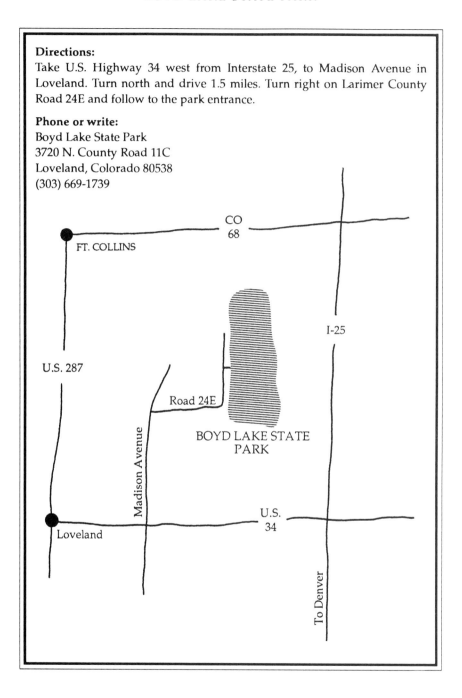

To the south of the campground is a natural area around Heinricy Lake, a small body of water outside the park boundary that is leased to the Division of Parks and Outdoor Recreation by the Greeley-Loveland Irrigation Company on a year-to-year basis. A trail begins at the small parking lot south of the campground and leads to the lake, then proceeds into Loveland. While enjoying a quiet, relaxing walk, the careful observer can pick out pheasants, hawks, pelicans, and several species of waterfowl from an old ditch-rider's trail along the east shoreline. The west side of the lake is privately owned.

Castlewood Canyon State Park

On the vast open prairie northeast of Colorado Springs lies a large upland plain often referred to as the Palmer Divide. This elevated land separates two watersheds: the Arkansas River to the south and the South Platte River to the north.

On the northern slope of this divide, Cherry Creek slices through the heart of Castlewood Canyon State Park. The canyon is an unexpected environment on the gentle, rolling hills of the prairie. The plant life here is more commonly found in the mountains than on the plains. Ponderosa pine, Douglas fir, juniper, thickets of gambel oak, and several stands of aspen thrive along the canyon floor.

The most prominent feature within the park boundaries, however, is man-made: the ruin of Castlewood Dam. This historic landmark had a tremendous impact on the history of Denver. Construction on the Castlewood Dam began on December 5, 1889, and was completed in November 1890. The project was undertaken by the Denver Land and Water Storage Company to improve the agricultural productivity of the surrounding area. But only six months after completion, the masonry structure developed a longitudinal fissure along the top. The crack, which was patched at the time, measured from a quarter of an inch to two inches wide. Despite the repairs, more cracks developed over time. The owners of the dam refused to accept responsibility, claiming that the dam had been built over a spring, which weakened it and caused the cracks.

Inspections of the dam were made in March 1890 and May 1891 by representatives of the city of Denver. The inspections revealed that the foundation was poorly constructed because a layer of clay and patches of quicksand covered the canyon floor. The weight of the dam on the unstable soil caused the structure to settle, creating the large fissures.

Castlewood Canyon State Park. The most prominent feature within the park boundaries is the ruin of Castlewood Dam. This historic landmark had a trememdous impact on the history of Denver.

On August 3, 1933, forty-three years after the dam had been built, a violent thunderstorm drenched the vicinity of Castlewood Canyon. The reservoir filled to capacity, and the additional weight forced water through the old crack. Hugh Paine, the dam's caretaker, made several attempts to release water through the control gates to relieve pressure on the trembling dam. Realizing that his efforts were useless, he set out to warn authorities about the failing structure. Unfortunately, the dam burst long before Paine reached Castle Rock.

At about 1:30 A.M. the dam collapsed, sending a thirty-foot wall of muddy water racing through the narrow canyon. The raging water ripped through the peaceful Cherry Creek Valley, ruining acres of fertile farmland, drowning scores of cattle and horses, and sweeping away several bridges. August Deepe, owner of the telephone exchange in Parker, was awakened by the switchboard activity of frightened citizens in the valley. At about 2:30 A.M. Deepe called authorities in Denver to alert them to the possible catastrophe. Denver policemen and fire-fighters heroically raced through the low-lying areas, warning people of the oncoming disaster. The crest of the flood reached Denver at 7:30 A.M. Approximately half an hour later, the swollen stream began receding.

The headlines of the August 3, 1933, edition of the *Denver Post* read, "Lower Section of Denver Flooded as Castlewood Dam Rips Out and Sends Deluge Down Cherry Creek." Basements of hundreds of homes and businesses were flooded in the lower part of the city. Water completely filled the subways at Denver's Union Station and stood a foot deep in the lobby. Damage in Denver alone was estimated to be $750,000; another $210,540 in damage occurred upstream. Miraculously, there were only two casualties during this devastating flood. Eighty-year-old Tom Casey was found floating in a large pool of water in his backyard after apparently falling into a deep hole while trying to flee the raging water; and Mrs. Bertha Catlin, age twenty-one, drowned in Cherry Creek while surveying the flood damage near Parker when the horse she was riding spooked and threw her into the swollen stream.

Located only thirty miles south of Denver, Castlewood Canyon State Park is a day-use park that stays open from sunrise to sunset. The 873-acre preserve became a state park in 1980. Although small, it contains steep colorful canyons, the meandering Cherry Creek, a waterfall, lush vegetation, and an abundance of wildlife. Lying in an ecologically unique setting, the park is used for a variety of activities, including picnicking, hiking, technical rock climbing, nature study, and nature photography.

The north entrance gate is located on Douglas County Road 51, which passes through the park between Cherry Creek and the west canyon wall. This road provides access to several trailheads and four parking areas with picnic sites. In the near future, a new main entrance gate (which is under construction) will be located along Colorado Highway 83 about six miles south of Franktown. A new visitor and nature center is also being built overlooking the majestic Castlewood Canyon. From the visitor center, a hiking trail will extend down into the canyon and join the existing system of nine trails. The trails form two loops, providing visitors with over five miles of canyon to explore.

Just south of the north gate is the trailhead to the Homestead Trail, an easy quarter-mile route that passes by the Old Lucas Homestead. The Pat Lucas family farmed the area during the early part of the century until the Great Depression. Although most early buildings were made of logs or built from wooden frames, this particular structure was made

Castlewood Canyon State Park. Just south of the north gate is the Old Lucas Homestead. Notice the walls of this old house, most early buildings were made from logs or built from wooden frames. This particular structure was made from concrete.

from concrete. The trail continues past the remains of several ranch buildings before joining the Rim Rock Trail and the Creek Side Trail.

The Creek Side Trail is a three-quarter-mile-long path that extends southward through dense thickets of gambel oak, passes through the picnic areas, and ends at the waterfall parking area, where it joins the Falls Trail. The picnic areas provide visitors with numerous tables and fire grills. There is no water available and just one vault toilet, the only one in the park.

The canyon walls below the falls still bear the scars of the flood of 1933. A cross section of the canyon shows a surface sheet of sandstone and conglomerates over 100 feet thick. Below this formation along the creek, the canyon floor contains a bed of clay consisting of 64 percent silica, 19 percent alumina, 6 percent iron, and some lime carbonate.

The half-mile Falls Trail skirts the waterfall and continues south-ward parallel to Cherry Creek. This trail ascends to the Dam Trail and ends at the old dam. Signs are posted warning visitors not to climb on this old masonry structure. The mortar is weak, creating unsafe climbing conditions.

Directions:
From Denver, take Colorado Highway 83 south to Franktown, turn west on Colorado Highway 86 for a fourth of a mile, then turn south on Douglas County Road 51 and drive 3 miles to the north entrance gate. Or take Interstate 25 to Castle Rock, follow Colorado 86 east for 6.75 miles to Douglas County 51, turn south and follow to the north entrance. Upon completion, the main entrance will be on Colorado 83, 6 miles south of Franktown.

Phone or write:
Castlewood Canyon State Park
Box 504
Franktown, Colorado 80116-0504
(303) 688-5242

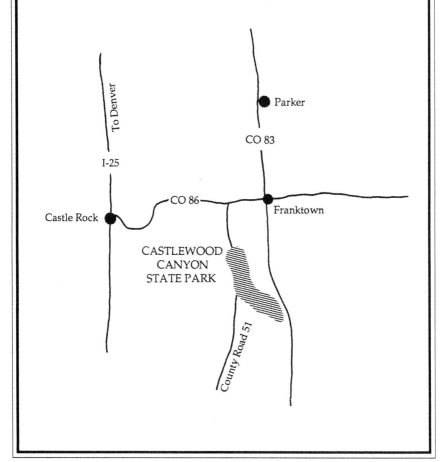

The Dam Trail, a steep quarter-mile footpath, starts on the west side of the dam next to the road. It drops down into the canyon, crosses Cherry Creek, and extends to the dam's east side, where it meets the Rim Rock Trail and the Inner Canyon Trail. From the east side of the canyon, hikers have a chance to study the interior of the dam and the stair-step pattern in which it was built.

Below scenic Canyon Point (which is a large rock outcrop overlooking the canyon) is the trailhead for the Rim Rock and Inner Canyon trails. The moderate 1.5-mile Rim Rock Trail climbs to the top of the east ridge and continues along it before returning to the Homestead Trail. At several places along the Rim Rock Trail, hikers are rewarded with majestic views of the canyon below, Pikes Peak to the south, and the Continental Divide to the west. Signs along the trail remind visitors that rattlesnakes inhabit the park. These reptiles normally shy away from people, however, they will strike when provoked. When it comes to snakes, pets are at greater risk than their owners and should be kept on a leash.

The Inner Canyon Trail is a moderate one-mile trail beginning at the junction of the Dam Trail and the Rim Rock Trail. It follows Cherry Creek eastward along the narrow canyon and meets the east trailhead of the Lake Gulch Trail, which climbs the south rim near the site of the future visitor center. It then drops back down into the canyon, forming a loop when it joins the Inner Canyon Trail, which returns to the Dam Trail.

The last two trails begin on the west side of the canyon near the picnic areas. The Climber's Trail and the Cave Trail are each a fourth of a mile long and rated moderate to steep. Both lead to the base of a sandstone cliff along the west ridge. These vertical walls provide a challenge for technical rock climbers wanting to perfect their skills. The palisade at the end of the Climber's Trail is known as Grocery Store Wall. At the end of the Cave Trail, about fifty feet above the base of the cliff, explorers will find the entrance to a small cave. Unfortunately, the only people who can get to this opening are people with rock-climbing ability.

While hiking any of these trails, the careful observer may see a variety of wildlife. Coyotes, squirrels, rabbits, and an occasional bobcat may be seen along Rim Rock Trail. The canyon walls provide an ideal nesting habitat for birds, including falcons and hawks. Visitors are often amazed to see turkey vultures riding the thermals above them.

Chatfield State Park

Many of the early explorers and settlers in Colorado were stricken with gold fever. In July 1858 William G. Russell and a small band of hopefuls exploring the South Platte River found gold near the mouth of present-day Little Dry Creek. Gold had been found previously along Clear Creek near today's Arvada, and along Cherry Creek. Although this new placer strike yielded only a few hundred dollars in gold, it helped ignite the Colorado gold rush. When word of the discovery reached the newspapers in Kansas City, prospectors and fortune hunters migrated west by the thousands, each expecting to find instant wealth and fame.

The gold fever was short-lived, though. As the rush came to an end, agriculture became the dominant way of life. The newcomers built their homes and established businesses along the banks of the South Platte. The Indians, with their knowledge of the land, warned the pioneers not to put their dwellings up along the river, claiming that the gods would be angry; it was "bad medicine" to build along the river. The settlers scoffed and ignored the advice.

Denver was only five years old when the warning of bad medicine came true. In 1864 heavy rains sent a fifteen-foot wall of water roaring through the city. The flood swept away a sawmill, a church, a newspaper office, the Lawrence Street Bridge, and hundreds of homes. Nineteen deaths were recorded in this catastrophe.

Floodwaters rumbled through the Denver area again in 1876, 1885, and 1894. The next flood did not occur until 1933, followed by one in 1935 and another in 1942. Then on June 6, 1965, the gods were angry once more. A flash flood in the foothills southwest of Denver sent water rushing down Plum Creek toward the South Platte River and metropolitan Denver. The result: over $300 million in damage to homes and businesses.

In August 1967, two years after the calamitous flood, the U.S. Army Corps of Engineers began constructing the Chatfield Dam as a flood control measure, completing the job in 1976. Construction on the recreational facilities began in 1973; in 1974 the property was leased to the Colorado Division of Parks and Outdoor Recreation. Total cost of the Chatfield project came to just over $100 million.

Chatfield State Park (formerly Chatfield State Recreation Area) was named after Issac W. Chatfield, who was a Union lieutenant in the Civil War. Chatfield purchased 720 acres of land near the confluence of the South Platte River and Plum Creek in 1870 and farmed the land until he moved in 1879. His property is now part of a 5,378-acre park that offers approximately thirty outdoor activities and draws more than 1.5 million visitors each year.

An interesting place to begin exploring Chatfield is the U.S. Army Corps of Engineers Visitor Center on the west side of the park. Seen from here, the reservoir resembles a large horseshoe, with the South Platte flowing in from the southwest, and Plum Creek entering from the southeast. Large photo displays that cover the walls illustrate the history of the South Platte River and how the dam was put up. People are always fascinated by the large fossilized mammoth skull that was discovered during excavation of the spillway on October 4, 1971. The skull was found fifty feet below ground level and later identified by a team from the Branch of Paleontology and Stratigraphy of the U.S. Geological Survey. Mammoths roamed the earth during the Pleistocene Epoch some 100,000 years ago and became extinct in North America roughly 10,000 years ago.

Fishing and water sports are the most prevalent activities at Chatfield. The 1,450-acre lake is periodically stocked with rainbow trout, crappie, yellow perch, catfish, bluegill, carp, and bass. There is a fifteen-inch minimum size limit on largemouth bass to allow the young fish time to mature. The best fishing at Chatfield takes place during the cool morning and evening hours. Ice fishing is popular during the winter months.

Just west of the marina, a fishing pier provides safe, secure fishing for handicapped visitors. The gently sloping shoreline is also handicapped-accessible from the marina to Plum Creek. A cement nature and fishing trail runs along the riparian zone of the South Platte River at the southwest section of the park. This trail was made possible by the

Chatfield State Park. The modern Chatfield Marina offers boat and slip rentals, fuel, fishing accessories, and a food concession.

Boettcher and Gates foundations through Opportunities for Handicapped Sportsmen Inc., and the Mission Viejo Company. The swim beach, picnic areas, and campgrounds are also handicapped-accessible.

Boating, waterskiing, sailing, jet skiing, windsurfing, and swimming are among the most popular recreations at Chatfield during the hot summer months. To avoid conflict and congestion, no more than 400 vessels are allowed to launch at a time. Some activities are restricted to certain areas of the lake. Denverites flock to the beach located along the west shoreline to soak up the warm Colorado sun. A volleyball court, picnic area, food concession, and first-aid station flank the beach. In addition, three boat ramps serve the reservoir. Two are located along the northern tip of the lake directly below the dam. The third ramp is next to the Chatfield Marina on the eastern shore. This modern marina offers slip rentals, boat rentals, fuel, and food. Jet skis, water skis, and sailboards are also available on a rental basis.

Two other well-liked activities at Chatfield are nature study and wildlife photography. Over 180 species of birds have been identified at Chatfield, including red-tailed hawks, great horned owls, cormorants, and a large variety of waterfowl and shorebirds. The most popular bird at Chatfield among bird watchers is the great blue heron. These magnificent creatures have nested in the tall cottonwood trees on the southwest side of the reservoir for over eighty years. More than fifty pairs of great blue herons have been counted in the twenty-seven-acre rookery. The largest wading birds in Colorado, they stand four to five feet tall and have a wing span of six feet. Herons migrate into Colorado in March, start their courtship, and begin nest building. Herons usually lay two to five eggs during a two-week period, with both parents incubating the eggs; the first chick hatches in about twenty-eight days. In September the birds begin their migration back to Texas and Mexico. Each year several of the old trees fall into the water, and with the loss of valuable nesting sites, the herons are gradually moving their nests further south to a clump of cottonwoods near the South Platte.

Herons are hardly the only wildlife in the park. By hiking through the riparian zone of the South Platte River in the early morning or evening hours, the careful observer can find mule deer, porcupines, rabbits, squirrels, and a variety of birds. On the east side of the park, a nature trail follows Plum Creek to a densely wooded place with a number of small ponds that support several species of frogs and box turtles. Numerous species of birds can also be identified along the creek.

Equestrians will find nearly twenty-four miles of trails that extend from the Chatfield Livery Stables along the South Platte into Waterton Canyon, which is the trailhead of the famous Colorado Trail. The stables, located on the west side of the park, offer riding lessons and rent horses at an hourly rate. Arrangements can be made for hay rides, breakfast rides, barbecue rides, and sleigh rides for families and groups. The stables are home to Chatfield's Belgian hitch horses, which are presented in horse shows, parades, and special events. Future plans include expanding the stables to provide boarding of private horses. The new facilities would also have an indoor and outdoor arena. The stables are open year-round. However, reservations are required during the winter months.

Physical fitness buffs such as bicyclists, joggers, and walkers share approximately seventeen miles of paved trails that meander through the park. Cross-country skiers can take advantage of the same trails during winter if snow permits. Dogs can get a workout, too; northwest of the dam, a wooded area is available for people wanting to exercise their dogs and provide obedience training.

Chatfield State Park. Just north of the west entrance is the Montgolfier Launch Site. This launch site was built and is maintained through a joint effort by the Colorado Division of Parks and Outdoor Recreation and the Chatfield Balloon Port Association.

Aviation hobbyists find Chatfield to their liking. Model airplane enthusiasts congregate at the Chatfield Aerodrome on the south side of the park. This airplane field, built and maintained by the Jeffco Aeromodelers Club and the Division of Parks and Outdoor Recreation, is open to the public. Membership in the Jeffco Aeromodelers Club is not required. Balloonists, meanwhile, head for the Montgolfier Launch Site just north of the west entrance. The Division of Parks and Outdoor Recreation and the Chatfield Balloon Port Association built the site. A ballooning permit is required to launch. Early risers may witness a splendid scene as the colorful balloons rise up and over the sparkling water.

Families can enjoy the numerous picnic sites scattered around the reservoir. All sites have tables and grills. There are three sites near the South Platte north of the dam: Owl Glen, Stevens Grove, and Cotton-wood Grove. On the west side of the reservoir is the Massey Draw picnic site. The three covered tables at the overlook on top of the dam provide a colorful view of the lake and the foothills to the south and west and the Denver skyline to the north. Along the west shore are the Jamison and

Directions:
From Denver, go south on Wadsworth Boulevard to Colorado Highway 121. Continue south, and turn east into the Deer Creek entrance. Or follow Santa Fe Drive south to Titan Road, turn west and go to Roxborough Park Road; turn north and go to the Plum Creek entrance.

Phone or write:
Chatfield State Park
11500 N. Roxborough Park Road
Littleton, Colorado 80125
(303) 791-7275
Chatfield Marina: (303) 791-7547
Chatfield Livery Stables: (303) 978-9898

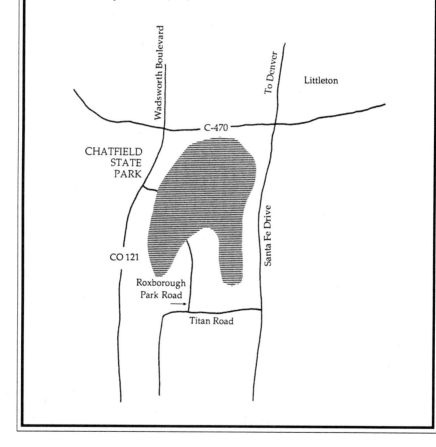

Catfish Flats picnic sites. A small picnic site with a volleyball court is on the east side of the park beside Plum Creek. Three group picnic areas can be reserved for weekends: Marina Point next to the marina, Heron Overlook on the south side next to the rookery, and Fox Run located along the west shore.

Three camping loops provide 153 campsites suitable for tents, trailers, pickup campers, and motor homes. Each campsite is equipped with a table and grill. Flush toilets, showers, water hydrants, laundry facilities, and a playground are conveniently located throughout the campground. The fifty-one sites in Loop A have electrical hookups. To the south of the campground is a large group campsite that can be reserved in advance. At the amphitheater located between Loop A and Loop B, park rangers and naturalists provide slide lecture programs about the geology, history, and wildlife of the park and surrounding area. These programs are presented from Memorial Day through Labor Day on weekend evenings. On request, park rangers will also lead visitors of all ages on interpretive nature walks.

Cherry Creek State Park

Standing in the pull-off area on Cherry Creek Dam Road, one gazes down onto the multicolored sailboats skimming across the sparkling water. The modern skyline of Denver stands on the horizon, while the foreground is filled by the thousands of homes and businesses that encircle the Cherry Creek State Park (formerly Cherry Creek State Recreation Area). It's hard to imagine that this area was once part of the famous Smoky Hill Trail that carried early pioneers on their westward journey.

The Smoky Hill Trail began as an old Indian trail across Kansas. It was named after large sandstone mounds northwest of Salina. They were known as the Smoky Hills, because a natural haze often covered them in the early morning hours. During the gold rush, pioneers wanted a shorter, faster route to the goldfields of Colorado. Despite the scarcity of water, scorching sun, and the threat of hostile Indians, the trail got plenty of traffic. Travelers began from several locations along the Missouri River, including Kansas City; Leavenworth, Kansas; and Westport, Missouri. The trail ended at the present day intersection of Broadway and Colfax in the heart of downtown Denver. It was replaced in 1870 by the Union Pacific Railroad.

The trail was used by the Wells Fargo Express and the Butterfield Overland Despatch, which carried stagecoaches loaded with supplies and passengers across the dusty plains. Between 1859 and 1865, thousands of pioneers reached the goldfields via the Smoky Hill Trail. Riders could board the stage and drivers could change horses at numerous stage stations along the trail. Two of these famous sites lie within the Cherry Creek State Park boundary. One station, the Nine Mile House, was a small cabin approximately nine miles from downtown Denver near the junction of the Middle Smoky Hill Trail and Smoky Hill South Stage Route. The site of Nine Mile House now lies beneath Cherry Creek Reservoir, near the outlet. Another stage station, the Twelve Mile House, gained fame for its large hotel and barroom operated by Johnnie Melvin. Melvin took pride in supplying a fresh team of four white horses to each stagecoach for its final run into Denver. Twelve Mile House stood on the open grassy plains in the southeast section of the park. Members of the Cherry Creek Valley Historical Society have studied the area but have recovered no artifacts.

During the first half of this century, the vast open plains experienced a period of slow growth. The area south and east of Denver was used for farming, with the lands along Cherry Creek among the richest. The old stage stops along the Smoky Hill Trail vanished; the only settlements that remain are the communities of Parker, Franktown, Elizabeth, and Kiowa.

Prior to 1946 Cherry Creek flooded occasionally, threatening southeast Denver. In 1946 the U.S. Army Corps of Engineers began constructing the Cherry Creek Dam, completing it in 1950 at a cost of $14 million.

On June 17, 1959, Governor Stephen McNichols signed a twenty-five-year lease with the Corps of Engineers allowing Colorado to obtain Cherry Creek State Recreation Area as the first unit of the new state park system. Cherry Creek is now a 4,715-acre complex that offers over thirty outdoor activities and receives more than 1.3 million visitors each year.

Fishing is one of the primary activities at Cherry Creek. The 880-acre lake is stocked with trout, bass, catfish, crappie, and walleye; it holds the state record for the largest walleye caught — sixteen pounds, eight ounces and thirty-four inches long. The Tower Loop area on the east side and the shore along the dam are favorite fishing spots for anglers. The Mountain Loop and Prairie Loop areas along the west shore are also known for good fishing. Special facilities along the east shore near the boat ramps can accommodate handicapped fishermen. Dixon Grove on the east shore and the Mountain Loop area on the west side are open to handicapped guests, as are the swim beach, picnic areas, and campground.

The beach along the east shore is a favorite summer destination for Denverites, who soak up the warm Colorado sun while viewing snow-capped mountain peaks. The beach features a volleyball court, food concessions, a picnic area, and a first-aid station. Water sports include

Cherry Creek State Park. On the rolling hills on the west side of the park is a large prairie dog colony. These sociable rodents can be observed and photographed year-round.

sailing, waterskiing, jet skiing, rowing, and windsurfing. To avoid conflict and congestion, no more than 350 vessels are allowed to launch at a time. Some activities are restricted to specific areas of the lake.

Two boat ramps and a large parking lot for trailers also lie on the east shore. Directly south of the boat ramps is another beach area, where jet skis can be rented. Sailboard rentals, along with sailboarding and rowing lessons, are offered at the Lake Loop area on the west side of the reservoir. And the Cherry Creek Marina near the west entrance station offers boat rental, slip rental, fuel, and boating accessories, with food and beverages on sale at the concession building next door.

Those who prefer dry land to water may engage in nature study and wildlife photography. The rolling hills of the west side of the park support a large prairie dog colony. These sociable rodents can be observed and photographed year-round. With a little luck, one might see burrowing owls, which often reside in abandoned prairie dog dens. More wildlife is visible from a nature trail leading from the Prairie Loop area along the southwest shore through clusters of willows and cattails.

Ducks, geese, and white pelicans are frequently seen; with a pair of binoculars or a spotting scope, cormorants can be observed roosting on the few remaining cottonwood trees in the south end of the reservoir.

From the parking lot at the south end of the park, several more trails extend north and south into the thick bushes and cottonwoods that thrive along Cherry Creek. This densely wooded area is amazingly quiet, although on weekends it often gets crowded. During the week, however, it can pass for a remote wilderness. Numerous birds, including great horned owls, make their nests in the tall cottonwoods. In the early morning and evening, cottontail rabbits, squirrels, fox, and deer can be observed and photographed throughout the park.

Future plans include building the Cherry Creek Trail, a thirty-two-mile trail that will follow Cherry Creek from the reservoir to Castlewood Canyon. This project will be a joint effort between Arapahoe and Douglas counties, the cities of Aurora and Parker, and the Colorado Division of Parks and Outdoor Recreation.

In 1990 the Denver Earth Day committee developed a unique project with long-lasting effects. Terry Brown, tree planting coordinator for the committee, and several hundred volunteers planted 3,000 trees on the grassy plains of the park's west side. The volunteers planted 1,000 plum trees in the shape of letters spelling "EARTH DAY 90." Each letter is seventy feet from end to end. After the letters were completed, 2,000 Russian olive trees were planted around them. The committee hopes that by Earth Day 2000 the trees will be mature enough so that the letters can be read from the air.

Speaking of the air, model airplane enthusiasts will find an airplane field with two paved runways on the west side of the park. The field was built in 1978 and is maintained by park rangers and the Denver R/C Eagles Club. The airstrip is open to the public; membership in the R/C Eagles Club is not required.

A public outdoor shooting range sits in the southwest part of the park, just off Jordan Road. Operated by the Cherry Creek Gun Club, the range has bull's-eye targets of twenty-five, fifty, and one hundred yards for rifles and pistols, along with skeet shooting for shotguns. The club periodically offers firearm safety classes and shooting lessons. Each participant must furnish his or her own firearm. The range is open March 1 through November 30.

People wanting to train their dogs for hunting can use the training

Cherry Creek State Park. On the west side of the park, model airplane enthusiasts will find an airplane field with two runways. The field was built in 1978 and is maintained by park rangers and the Denver R/C Eagles Club.

grounds in the park's southeast section along Parker Road. Hunters must supply their own birds for the training and use shotguns with bird shot or blanks; they may not hunt wild mammals or birds.

Equestrians are delighted to find that the park has approximately ten miles of trails along Cherry Creek. The Paint Horse Stables located near the east gate entrance rent horses by the hour on a first-come, first-serve basis. The stables give riding lessons, board private horses, and offer hay rides and sleigh rides for families and youth groups. They are open seven days a week, May through September, and on weekends during the winter.

In their quest for physical fitness, bicyclists, joggers, and walkers share eight miles of paved trails that meander around the reservoir and across the grassy plains. Cross-country skiers can take advantage of the same trails during winter.

Families can relax in the shade of tall cottonwood trees at the Dixon Grove picnic area. Numerous sheltered picnic sites with tables and grills are situated on the east and west shores. There are four group picnic areas that can be reserved in advance; Dixon Grove, Smoky Hill Shelter,

Directions:
Go 1 mile south of Interstate 225 on Parker Road and turn west on Lehigh Avenue to enter the park.

Phone or write:
Cherry Creek State Park
4201 S. Parker Road
Aurora, Colorado 80014
(303) 699-3860

Cherry Creek Gun Club: (303) 693-1765
Paint Horse Stables: (303) 690-8235
Cherry Creek Marina: (303) 779-6144
Rocky Mountain Jet Ski: (303) 766-0766

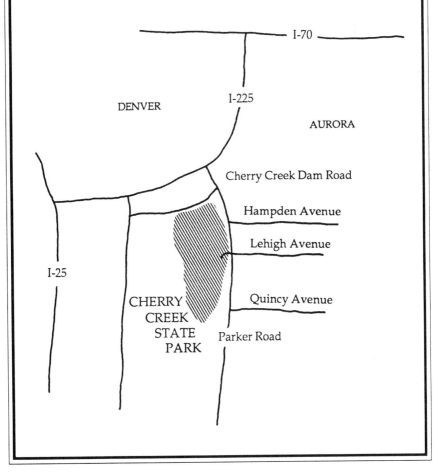

and Twelve Mile, all located along the east of the lake, and the Hobie Hill site on the west side near the marina.

Cherry Creek's large campground, located on the east side of the park, has 102 campsites for tents, campers, and motor homes. Each site is equipped with a table and grill; electrical hookups are not available. Additional facilities include flush toilets, showers, laundry, water hydrants, a soft drink machine, and a public phone. Campers are advised to bring their own firewood.

The Cherry Creek Basin Water Quality Authority was created by the Colorado legislature in 1988 to develop and carry out a plan to reduce the algae in Cherry Creek Reservoir. The algae creates no health concerns for swimmers or boaters, and fish caught in the reservoir are safe to eat. In fact, several species of fish rely on algae for survival. However, the abundance of algae in the reservoir depletes the oxygen supply in the water, posing a long-term threat.

As part of the algae-control effort, the water quality authority, in cooperation with the city of Aurora, has developed the Shop Creek Project on the east side of the reservoir. This man-made wetlands traps silt from urban stormwater in storage ponds along Shop Creek. Silt contains nutrients that support algae; it also fills the bottom of the reservoir and reduces the amount of water it can hold. By reducing the amount of silt that reaches the reservoir, the Shop Creek Project helps maintain a large water-storage capacity and reduces the proliferation of algae.

To fund these activities, the authority has authorized an additional fee of $3.00 per car per year for annual park passes, or $1.00 per car for day passes. Annual pass holders receive a decal to place on the windshield next to the Colorado State Parks Pass.

Colorado State Forest State Park

Awesome, magnificent, spectacular — these are just a few of the many words used to express the beauty of Colorado State Forest State Park. Located in northern Colorado along the eastern edge of North Park, Colorado State Forest is truly one of Colorado's most scenic areas. Even people who visit the area on a regular basis find the mountain scenery breathtaking.

Colorado State Forest is a 70,768-acre preserve that extends thirty miles from north to south along the western slope of the Medicine Bow Mountains and into the Never Summer range. The Colorado State Forest is flanked on the west by a vast open basin and on the east by the Rawah Wilderness. Elevations vary from 8,400 feet along the western border to the 12,951-foot Clark Peak. With this range in elevation, visitors have the chance to explore three of earth's life zones: montane, subalpine, and alpine tundra.

The Medicine Bow range is the result of localized movements of the earth's crust that took place when the entire region was thrust upward during the birth of the Rocky Mountains. Folding and faulting below the earth's surface created the force behind the uplift, which lasted over several million years toward the end of the Mesozoic Era. Most of the peaks and U-shaped valleys of the Colorado State Forest were carved by widespread glacial activity that occurred approximately 75,000 years ago. As the glaciers receded, they left deep bowls below the towering peaks.

The North Park area was originally inhabited by the Ute Indians. Occasionally the Arapahoe, Cheyenne, Crow, and Sioux would venture into the open valley in search of game. In the nineteenth century, hundreds of fur trappers explored the mountains of the North Park region looking for animal skins, especially beaver pelts, which could bring top

57

dollar in the eastern states. The abundance of wildlife was a bonanza for many hunters. Two famous explorers, John Charles Fremont and Kit Carson, ventured into North Park in 1843 and described it as a "beautiful circular valley."

In the early 1870s, prospectors rushed to the North Park vicinity to establish their claims on the rich ore hidden in the mountains. Only a few mine shafts and skeletal frames of buildings in ghost towns remain. Teller City, which lies south of the state forest boundary, is the most prominent of the remaining ghost towns. As the mining industry died out during the late 1870s, farming and ranching began to spread across North Park. In 1879 a drought on the high plains of eastern Colorado forced ranchers to move their herds into the area. Stockmen were confident that their cattle could survive the long winters. Unfortunately, the winter of 1883–1884 was devastating. Nearly half of the stock died of starvation. These early ranchers learned to save an abundance of hay as cattle feed for the long winter months.

With the disappearance of mining, North Park settled into a long, stable period of slow growth. Ranching emerged as the dominant industry, and timber cutting also became an important part of the local economy. The region remained isolated from the population centers of the Front Range, however, attracting relatively few visitors.

Colorado State Forest was created through a land exchange between the Colorado Board of Land Commissioners and the U.S. Forest Service. The exchange was completed December 2, 1938, when President Franklin D. Roosevelt issued a patent to Colorado for 70,980 acres. In 1953 the state legislature designated this section of land the Colorado State Forest. It was not until 1970 that the Colorado State Forest became a state park. At that time an agreement was reached between the Colorado Game, Fish and Parks Department and the Board of Land Commissioners, which agreed to lease the land for recreational use. In 1972 the Colorado Division of Parks and Outdoor Recreation was formed and continued the lease agreement.

Colorado State Forest is unique in that the park generates money for another state agency. Under the 1938 land trade agreement and Colorado law, the park is designated as a source of revenue for Colorado's public schools. The land is leased for timber cutting and cattle grazing, which bring in money for the schools.

The park is beloved more for its beauty than for its earnings, though. The spectacular scenery of the Colorado State Forest includes numerous mountain peaks, lakes, and landmarks with unusual names and colorful histories. The state forest is divided into several zones to provide better management and control. The most accessible and most used areas are in the southern half of the park.

The Middle Fork Zone follows a scenic corridor created by Colorado Highway 14 as it passes through the south end of the park. The corridor is bounded on the north by the Gould Mountain ridge, Diamond Peaks, and Cameron Pass. On the south side lies the riparian zone along the Middle Fork of the Michigan River, the Crags Scenic Area, and the northern tip of the Never Summer range.

Cameron Pass was named after General Robert A. Cameron. Cameron moved to Colorado in 1870 and became superintendent of the Union Colony (now Greeley). He was in charge of recruiting and greeting colonists. In 1870 Cameron explored the headwaters of the Cache la Poudre River. Nearby Cameron Pass was named for him by Union Pacific Railroad surveyors. In 1882 a toll road to Teller City opened. The road was improved for automobile use in 1926 and paved in 1979.

The Crags Scenic Area looms high above Colorado 14 in the northern edge of the Never Summer Mountains. The jagged edges of the Nokhu Crags rise 12,485 feet above sea level and are considered the most dramatic landmark in Colorado State Forest. In 1914 the Colorado Geographical Board abbreviated the original Arapahoe name, *Neaha-no-xhu* (meaning "eagle's nest"), to Nokhu Crags.

Near the base of Cameron Pass on Colorado 14, Lake Agnes Road extends southward across the Michigan River to the beginning of the Lake Agnes Trail. An old rustic cabin that was once part of a boys' camp stands near the trailhead. Unfortunately, a young boy drowned in the lake, and the camp never reopened. The cabin is one of seven in the park available on a rental basis.

The most popular hiking trail in the park, the Lake Agnes Trail, is a short but difficult route leading to the edge of a large glacier bowl that holds the lake. It was originally called Island Lake, then renamed by John Zimmerman in honor of one of his daughters. (Zimmerman owned the once-famous Keystone Hotel along the upper Cache la Poudre River. In 1946 the state bought the property and built a fish-retaining pond.) The deep blue water of Lake Agnes lies below the west side of Nokhu Crags. To the south rises 12,940-foot Mount Richthofen, which sits on the northwestern edge of Rocky Mountain National Park; to the west looms 11,453-foot Seven Utes Mountain. The Arapahoes called this mountain

"Where-the-Arapahoe-killed-seven-Utes"; the name was shortened by the Colorado Geographical Board.

The American Lakes sit on the east side of Nokhu Crags, on the alpine tundra. The lakes can be reached by hiking the five-mile trail that begins along Lake Agnes Road and meanders through the subalpine forest and up above the timberline. The trail eventually crosses over Thunder Pass and into Rocky Mountain National Park. Anyone wishing to continue into the national park must obtain a National Park Service backcountry permit.

American Lakes can also be reached from Lake Agnes by following an old irrigation ditch that extends around the north side of Nokhu Crags and meets the American Lakes Trail. This ditch was designed in 1883 and built in 1888 by a group of ranchers near Fort Collins who wanted to divert water from Lake Agnes over Cameron Pass and into the Cache la Poudre. The ditch is seven miles long and drops 100 feet in elevation from the lake to Cameron Pass.

Next to the Ranger Lakes Campground is the Ranger Lakes Nature Trail. It is a half-mile trail with twelve interpretive stations that illustrate the flora, fauna, and ecological processes of Colorado State Forest. Near the trailhead, the trail divides. The main fork turns to the right and meanders through the dense pine forest to the campground. The other heads south to the lakes and becomes a fishing-access trail. Both forks are accessible to handicapped visitors.

The Glacial Cirques Scenic Area in the southern half of the park extends from just south of Clark Peak northward to North Rawah Peak. This area's open valleys and lush green meadows filled with wildflowers border the rugged peaks of the Medicine Bow Mountains. The name Medicine Bow derives from an Indian legend about friendly Indian tribes that met to make bows and arrows for hunting. The chiefs asked the gods for their blessings, believing these mountains were a place where the spirit could be uplifted and cast into heaven by magic, or "medicine." The Rawah Wilderness Area, on the eastern slope of the Medicine Bow Mountains, also takes its name from Native American culture. Rawah is an Indian word meaning "wilderness."

The Glacial Cirques area is reserved for hiking and fishing. Over ten miles of trails lead to the deep blue waters of several alpine lakes, including Ruby Jewel, Clear, and Kelly lakes, all situated high in the Medicine Bow Mountains. The most accessible of the lakes is Ruby

Colorado State Forest State Park. Jackson County Road 41 leads into the Glacial Cirques area of the Medicine Bow Mountains. This area provides over ten miles of hiking trails that lead to several alpine lakes, including Ruby Jewel, Kelly, and Clear lakes.

Jewel, located below Clark Peak. Kelly Lake was named after an old prospector who lived in a small cabin nearby. Kelly usually made several trips into Walden during the winter for supplies. Late one spring after a harsh winter, his body was found in his cabin by other explorers. Kelly's body and cabin were burned to cleanse the site.

To reach the Glacial Cirques Scenic Area, follow Jackson County Road 41, which begins at Colorado 14 next to the KOA campground along the park's western boundary. Jackson County 41 passes through the park entrance and follows the North Fork of the Michigan River beyond the North Michigan Reservoir (which is the largest body of water in the state forest) to an open valley where the road divides. The road on the right leads to the Bockman Campground; the one on the left continues north for approximately five miles to the Kelly Lake and Clear Lake trailheads. The trailhead to Ruby Jewel Lake begins about one mile north of the junction.

From the Bockman Campground, a four-wheel-drive road extends southward to Montgomery Pass. This old logging road ascends high

Colorado State Forest State Park. The North Sand Hills Recreation Area is located near the northern tip of the Colorado State Forest. This is a popular site for visitors to pursue the thrill of driving ATVs and motorized trail bikes over the dunes and through the deep bowls created by drifting sand.

above timberline to a spectacular 360-degree panorama of the Rawah Wilderness, Colorado State Forest, the Medicine Bow range, and the Never Summer Mountains.

The northern half of Colorado State Forest is undeveloped and seldom visited. This region is primarily used for hunting, backpacking, and logging. This semiwilderness has unique geological features and is divided into two zones. The 18,000-acre Ute Pass-Muddy Park Zone extends from Ute Pass southward to Clear Creek. An unusual feature of the Muddy Pass Zone is the East Sand Hills, approximately 640 acres of light-colored sand. Most of the dunes are dormant, with grasses, sage-brush, and trees scattered across the sand, creating a delicate ecosystem. This area is accessible only by foot and has been designated a Colorado Natural Area by the Department of Natural Resources.

North of the Muddy Park Zone is the Medicine Bow Divide Zone. This area also features sand dunes. The North Sand Hills Recreation Area is popular with recreationists who pursue the thrill of driving ATVs and motorized trail bikes across the dunes and through the deep bowls created by the drifting sand. These sand hills evolved over thousands of years as the winds carried granules across North Park and deposited them against the western edge of the Medicine Bow Mountains. The North Sand Hills can be reached via North Sand Hills Road, which begins just north of Cowdrey.

The northern portion of Colorado State Forest is crisscrossed by numerous four-wheel-drive roads. The most notable are the primitive trails to Ute Pass and Coon Peak. These old roads are rarely used and not maintained. Drivers exploring this territory do so at their own risk. Vehicles are required to stay on designated roads to prevent damage to the natural resources.

Many visitors to Colorado State Forest enjoy photographing and observing wildlife. In 1978 moose were reintroduced to the North Park area. These huge creatures are thriving and often seen in and around willow thickets on the Michigan River. The state forest supports large numbers of deer and elk, along with bighorn sheep that can be observed in their summer and winter ranges. Other mammals in the park include beavers, coyotes, black bears, marmots, and rabbits. Over 120 species of birds have been identified in the park, the most common being the red-tailed hawk, raven, Clark's nutcracker, and Steller's jay.

Anglers appreciate the excellent stream and lake fishing. Kelly Lake is one of the few places in Colorado where visitors can fish for golden trout, a species introduced from California. The other lakes and streams contain native, brown, brook, rainbow, and cutthroat trout. Only artificial flies and lures are permitted. Boating is allowed only on North Michigan Reservoir; power boats must be used at wakeless speed (under ten miles per hour). The one boat ramp that serves the lake is located along the north shore.

The state forest provides 104 campsites in four separate campgrounds at different elevations. Numerous campsites are scattered around North Michigan Reservoir, each equipped with a table, a fire grill, and vault toilets. At the Bockman Campground, two miles northeast of the reservoir, most of the sites are nestled beneath tall pines with tables and fire rings. There is a vault toilet at the southwest corner of the campground.

The Ranger Lakes and Crags campgrounds are south of Colorado 14 in the Middle Fork Zone. The campsites at Ranger Lakes Campground are all sheltered by a mature pine forest and equipped with tables and fire rings. Additional facilities include vault toilets, a water

Directions:
Drive 75 miles west of Fort Collins on Colorado Highway 14 over Cameron Pass. From Walden, drive 20 miles southeast on Colorado 14.

Phone or write:
Colorado State Forest State Park
Star Route Box 91
Walden, Colorado 80480
(303) 723-8366

hydrant, and a dump station near the campground entrance. The Crags Campground lies on a hillside in the shadow of Nokhu Crags. Each campsite has a table and fire ring, with a vault toilet in place near the campground entrance. With the exception of the Crags Campground, all campgrounds can accommodate tents, trailers, pickup campers, and motor homes. Due to the steep road leading to the Crags camping area, trailers are prohibited. Backcountry camping is allowed at various locations throughout the park, including Ruby Jewel, Kelly, and Clear lakes. (No camping is allowed at Lake Agnes.)

Tucked away inside the state forest are seven rustic cabins that are available for rent year-round. One cabin sits at the Lake Agnes Trailhead, while the others are scattered around North Michigan Reservoir. Two of the cabins can house up to fifteen people; the other four can sleep up to six.

Over 100 miles of trails, including many back roads, are open to hikers, mountain bikers, and horseback riders. Groups may use the park for pack trips and horse camping. However, horses may not use the Lake Agnes Trail or stay in designated campgrounds. Horses can be rented on an hourly basis from the North Michigan Reservoir Stables. The park maintains an extensive trail system for winter activities, with over fifty miles of groomed snowmobiling trails and forty-five miles of cross-country skiing trails.

A popular addition to the trail system are the three yurts, circular Mongolian tents made of canvas with wooden floors. The yurts are heated by wood-burning stoves and can comfortably sleep six. These shelters lie three to four miles apart along the trail system. They have become a popular form of refuge for cross-country skiers in the winter and mountain bikers during the summer.

Crawford State Park

People can forget their fast-paced urban lives for a while and enjoy tranquility in a scenic mountainous setting on the Western Slope at Crawford State Park (formerly Crawford State Recreation Area). At an elevation of 6,600 feet, Crawford lies in a narrow basin between the West Elk Mountains to the east and the Gunnison Uplift to the west. The uplift continues rising to the rim of the Black Canyon of the Gunnison, only eight air miles away.

The scenic West Elk Mountains contain roughly 900 square miles of volcanic terrain consisting mostly of volcanic breccia and basalt. Saddle Mountain, Lands End Peak, and the Castles are old volcanos and laccoliths. The most notable landform, Needle Rock, lies northeast of the park. This distinctive outcrop is a volcanic plug that formed when lava inside the volcano solidified and hardened; over time, the softer layers of ash eroded away, exposing the plug. A skinny pillar of rock once extended above the base rock, hence the name Needle Rock. In 1923 an earthquake rumbled through the valley, and the needle fell. Today, the plug looks more like a mitten than a needle.

Crawford Reservoir, one of several reservoirs in the Colorado River Storage Project, was built and is owned by the U.S. Bureau of Reclamation. Prior to construction of the dam, the Bureau of Reclamation had to purchase parcels of land from several families living in the valley. Those that gave up their land (and their home, in some cases) include the Goodwin family, the Speck family, Leslie Savage, Leslie Bealle, and Bill Ayer. Completed in 1963, the lake is filled with water transported by canal from the Smith Fork River, plus runoff from Iron Creek, Clear Fork, and Muddy Creek. This 406-acre reservoir provides irrigation water for ranchers and farmers throughout the valley. The National Park Service

Crawford State Park. The main attraction at Crawford during the summer months is the fishing. The abundance of yellow perch, largemouth bass, catfish, and rainbow trout attracts anglers from throughout Colorado.

built the basic recreational facilities between 1963 and 1966, and Crawford Reservoir became a state park in 1967. The recreational facilities are managed by the Colorado Division of Parks and Outdoor Recreation.

Crawford State Park has been a valuable resource for the small community of Crawford. A survey conducted in 1988 by park management found that approximately 40 percent of the gross revenue of the town came as a direct result of the recreationists visiting Crawford State Park. Visitors to Crawford, a short one-mile drive north of the park, are often amazed to see local ranchers herding their cattle through the middle of town. Each year ranchers drive the cattle from the low valleys to the high mountain meadows for summer grazing. In autumn, prior to the big-game hunting season, the ranchers return the cattle to the valleys via the streets of Crawford.

The primary draw at Crawford is fishing. The abundance of yellow perch, largemouth bass, catfish, and rainbow trout attracts anglers from throughout Colorado. The lake is also a favorite place for waterskiing, jet skiing, and sailing. During the late autumn, big-game hunters use it as a

Crawford State Park. The Clear Fork Campground offers twenty-six campsites in a scenic mountain setting.

base camp. In winter, cold-weather devotees enjoy ice fishing, ice skating, snowmobiling, and some cross-country skiing.

Most of the recreational facilities are located on the lake's east shore along Colorado Highway 92. Three campgrounds provide fifty-four campsites that can accommodate tents, trailers, pickup campers, and motor homes. Electrical hookups are not available at any of these campsites.

Along the northeast side of the lake, a peninsula extends several hundred yards into the reservoir. Visitors will find the park office and information center just inside the entrance station. Facilities include the Peninsula Campground, which has sixteen campsites in the center of the peninsula. Three walk-in tent sites are located along the shore directly below the entrance station. Tables, grills, and flush toilets are available. At the far end of the peninsula, visitors will find a boat ramp that serves the lake, along with ample parking space for trailers and automobiles. A swim beach (with no attendants on duty) lies just southwest of the entrance station. Due to the 6,600-foot elevation, the water is still rather cool around Memorial Day. The water temperature gradually rises, and

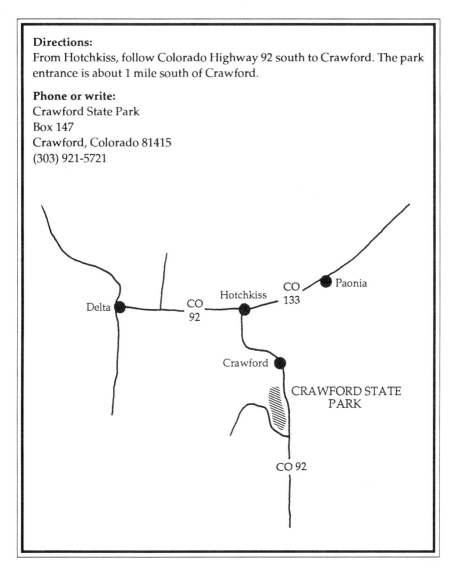

Directions:
From Hotchkiss, follow Colorado Highway 92 south to Crawford. The park entrance is about 1 mile south of Crawford.

Phone or write:
Crawford State Park
Box 147
Crawford, Colorado 81415
(303) 921-5721

by the middle of July it hits the mid-70s and remains quite pleasant for the rest of the summer.

A half-mile south of the peninsula is the Clear Fork Campground. It has twenty-six campsites with tables and grills, a volleyball court, a horseshoe pit, flush toilets, and a dump station. The Iron Creek Campground sits at the southeast corner of the lake, with nine campsites and a take-off/drop-off area for water-skiers.

The north side of the reservoir is strictly a day-use area. A road provides access to several picnic sites, each with tables, fire grills, and vault toilets. The road ends near the dam. From here, visitors have a scenic view of the reservoir to the south and the valley to the northwest below the dam. The north shore also provides a water ski take-off/drop-off area.

The Goodwin Cove day-use area along the west bank can be reached by taking Montrose County Road 3400 from Colorado 92. Upon entering Delta County, the road changes to Delta County Road B, which continues toward the north rim of the Black Canyon of the Gunnison. Goodwin Cove, primarily a shore-fishing access area with a few picnic tables and a pit toilet, also has the trailhead to the Indian Fire Nature Trail. This trail received its name after an event that happened to the Ute Indians in the late 1800s. The Utes occupied the area for centuries and were called the "blue sky people" by other Indian tribes. Their peaceful way of life came to an end as white settlers migrated into western Colorado. In 1881 the U.S. Cavalry forcibly removed the Native Americans to a reservation in Utah. This expulsion was called the "Trip of Sorrow." As the Utes were being ejected, they set fire to the land while white settlers watched from a distance, eagerly waiting for the chance to claim the land.

The trail is a half-mile self-guided path with ten interpretive markers that explain the plants, geology, and wildlife of the area. Visitors get the chance to examine the charred remains of several juniper trees that were burned during the exodus over 100 years ago.

Eldorado Canyon State Park

Two unusual things are apparent immediately upon entering Eldorado Canyon State Park. First, there is no paved road with hundreds of cars racing across it. In fact, Eldorado Canyon is one of few along the Front Range without a major highway. It has only a narrow dirt road that passes through a small parking lot before continuing to the park office and picnic grounds.

Second, the parking area is full of people carrying ropes strung over their shoulders with strange metal objects dangling from their waists. These people are rock climbers who have traveled to Eldorado Canyon to test their courage and skill on the canyon walls. Eldorado Canyon ranks with the Shawangunks in New York, Yosemite Valley in California, and Devils Tower in Wyoming as one of the best climbing areas in the United States. The first technical rock climbs in Eldorado occurred during the early 1950s. Now over 500 routes with names like Bastille Crack, Grand Giraffe, Wind Ridge, Ruper, and the Naked Edge attract climbers from almost every continent. These routes range from 5.0 to 5.13 in difficulty. Considering the number of climbers, there are few accidents at Eldorado. When an accident does occur, it can usually be attributed to inexperience or lack of respect for the sport.

The canyon walls were carved out of the 300-million-year-old Fountain Formation by South Boulder Creek as the land tilted skyward during the birth of the Rocky Mountains. Three main ridges rise above the creek to the north. The Red Garden Wall, the tallest ridge, towers 850 feet above the rushing stream, centered between Hawk Eagle Ridge to the east and the West Ridge on the west side. On the south side of South Boulder Creek is the Bastille, a vertical stone wall that juts abruptly above the narrow dirt road.

Eldorado Canyon State Park. Looking east from the rolling hills of Crescent Meadows, visitors can see the jagged edges of the Red Garden Wall of the Inner Canyon and the open plains beyond.

The canyon was first inhabited by the Ute Indians. The south-facing walls of the narrow canyon absorbed the warmth of the sun, offering protection from the harsh winters. It wasn't until the mid-1800s that white pioneers began settling in the region. In 1904 the small community of Eldorado Springs near the canyon entrance became known as a resort for the elite. Three thermal pools with 76-degree water and two plush hotels, the Eldorado and the Grand View, attracted such celebrities as John Barrymore and Jimmy Durante, as well as honeymooners Dwight and Mamie Eisenhower in 1915. Although the plush hotels were both destroyed by fire during the early part of the twentieth century, the town of Eldorado Springs still draws visitors who come to purchase the artesian springwater bottled there.

Eldorado Springs received considerable attention between 1906 and 1949 when Ivy Baldwin, a real adventurer for his time, performed tightrope acts across the canyon. Baldwin strung an inch-thick steel cable 672 feet between two rock formations, the Bastille on the south side of the canyon and the Wind Tower on the north side. On his first walk,

Directions:
From Boulder, drive 4 miles south on Colorado Highway 93, turn west on Colorado Highway 170 and drive 3 miles through Eldorado Springs to the park entrance. Crescent Meadows can be reached by automobile. From the junction of Colorado 93 and Colorado 72, drive west on Colorado 72 for 7.7 miles to Coal Creek. Turn right on Crescent Park Drive and follow the road up the hill to an intersection with Gross Dam Road. Turn right and continue for 1.7 miles across the railroad tracks to the park entrance.

Phone or write:
Eldorado Canyon State Park
Box B
Eldorado Springs, Colorado 80025
(303) 494-3943

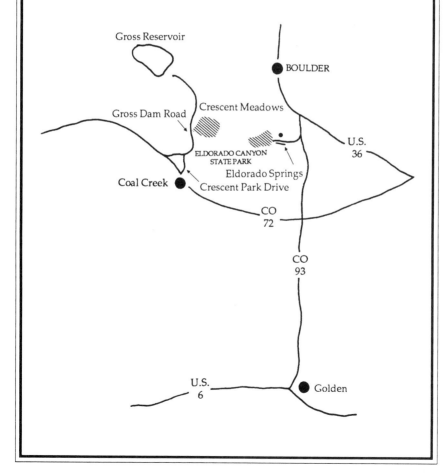

approximately 580 feet above the raging waters, he stopped and stood on his head. Over the years Baldwin performed his stunts eighty-nine times without safety nets. In 1949, on his eighty-second birthday, he stopped and knelt midway, to the cheers and applause of nearly 3,000 fans.

Eldorado Canyon became a state park in 1978. It is divided into two distinct areas. The 272-acre eastern portion, referred to as the Inner Canyon, is dominated by steep canyon walls covered with yellow and orange lichens. As the sun reflects off the lichens, it casts a golden hue across the canyon walls. This is how the canyon received the name Eldorado, Spanish for "golden" or "gilded one."

The Inner Canyon has several trails on which visitors can explore its natural beauty. An easy hike on the Streamside Trail along South Boulder Creek offers a good view of the rock climbers. The Rattlesnake Gulch Trail, a moderate 1.4-mile climb up the canyon walls, extends beyond the park boundary, to the ruins of the Crags Hotel. Built in 1908 on a ledge overlooking the canyon, the hotel was used as a whistle-stop by the Moffat Line Railroad. In November 1912 the luxurious building burned to the ground. Only segments of the foundation and the skeletal frame of a fireplace remain.

From the hotel ruins, the trail divides. A three-quarter-mile path extends south to the railroad tracks; the other fork travels west approximately a quarter of a mile to the scenic Continental Divide Overlook, which commands a magnificent view of the rugged canyon below and the high Rockies to the west. The trail continues to the railroad tracks and circles back to the ruins. The Rattlesnake Gulch Trail is the only trail in Eldorado available for mountain bikes. (The two-mile Fowler Trail, which branches off the Rattlesnake Gulch Trail a couple hundred yards from the trailhead, has been closed to the public because of a landslide.)

The longest and most difficult route, the Eldorado Canyon Trail, begins near the park office and picnic grounds at the park's western edge and extends 5.5 miles up and around private property to the second section of the park, Crescent Meadows. Most of the Eldorado Canyon Trail is open to horseback riding. However, portions are steep and narrow with large rocks in the path, creating an impassable situation for equestrians.

The 573-acre Crescent Meadows was obtained in 1979. It is distinctively different than the Inner Canyon, characterized by open, rolling hills covered with wildflowers during the spring and summer. Indian paintbrush, asters, penstemons, and mountain ball cactus are common to the region. Crescent Meadows is open to picnickers, (although there are no designated picnic areas or facilities), hikers, and anyone who cherishes the tranquility of open spaces. Camping is not allowed.

Those who enter the park on foot are required to purchase an individual walk-in pass for a nominal fee.

Eleven Mile State Park

Near the center of Colorado lies a vast 900-square-mile upland valley known as South Park. Ringed by mountains, the valley ranges in elevation from 8,500 to 10,000 feet above sea level. Archaeologists estimate that this region was first inhabited about 12,000 years ago. Evidence of the Folsom, Plano, Archaic, and Woodland prehistoric cultures has been discovered in South Park. The Ute Indians continued the lifestyle of earlier cultures, dominating all of the mountainous areas in Colorado as early as 1000 A.D. The Comanche, Kiowa, and later the Cheyenne and Arapahoe, all neighboring tribes from the plains, would occasionally raid the area, but for the most part the Utes controlled South Park and environs for several hundred years.

French fur trappers were the first white men to explore the territory, followed by the Spanish expeditions during the 1700s. Gold was discovered in Colorado in 1859, and the Colorado gold rush was on. The influx of speculators dramatically changed the land. Mines and mining towns supplanted the Ute hunting grounds. Several of those communities still exist in South Park, most notably Fairplay, along with Como, Jefferson, Hartsel, and Glentivar.

As the mining industry grew, so did the ranching and lumber industries. In time, these industries formed the backbone of the local economy. The mines played themselves out, the population leveled off, and South Park remained largely undeveloped.

In 1926 the Denver Board of Water Commissioners initiated survey work for a proposed dam at the point where the South Fork of the South Platte River leaves South Park and enters the confines of Eleven Mile Canyon. Construction began in August 1930. Upon completion of the dam in November 1932, the Eleven Mile Dam was hailed as an "engineering triumph." The 135-foot-high gravity-arch concrete dam was

Eleven Mile State Park. During the winter months, Eleven Mile traditionally provides some of the best ice fishing in Colorado. On any given weekend, it is not unusual to see 500 to 800 anglers on the frozen lake.

built on a series of stair-steps cut into each side of the canyon wall so that the walls, not the dam, held back the weight of the water.

Eleven Mile is now a 7,480-acre park with a 3,405-acre lake that provides approximately twenty-four miles of shoreline. It is located roughly forty miles west of Colorado Springs in the southeast corner of South Park. In August 1970 the Denver Board of Water Commissioners agreed to lease the recreational facilities to the Colorado Game, Fish and Parks Department. In 1972 the Colorado Division of Parks and Outdoor Recreation was founded and continued the lease agreement. Eleven Mile's limited facilities support two main activities, camping and fishing.

The north shore has six designated campgrounds: Stoll Mountain, Rocky Flats, Puma Hills, Ponderosa Ridge, Rocky Ridge, and North Shore. All campsites are equipped with tables and grills, with vault toilets and water hydrants near by. Stoll Mountain and Rocky Flats do not have water hydrants. A dump station is located near the North Shore entrance. North Shore also provides a children's playground and an amphitheater. On summer weekends — especially holiday weekends — park rangers and naturalists give lecture programs about the history, geology, and wildlife of the park and surrounding area.

Eleven Mile State Park. While their parents are ice fishing, children develop their own entertainment.

Five more campgrounds lie along the south shore: Cross Creek, Lazy Boy, Rocking Chair, Howbert Point, and Witcher Cove. Tables, grills, and vault toilets are provided at all of the campgrounds. Witcher Cove also has a water hydrant and a dump station near the entrance. All of these campgrounds can accommodate tents, campers, trailers, and motor homes. However, electrical hookups are not available.

A backcountry campground along the northeast shore offers twenty-five primitive sites. This area can be reached by a half-mile hike or by boat.

Fishing is the main attraction at Eleven Mile. Record-sized brown and rainbow trout, mackinaw, kokanee salmon, pike, and carp are abundant in the reservoir. During the winter months, Eleven Mile traditionally provides some of the best ice fishing in Colorado. On any given weekend, it is not unusual to see 500 to 800 people fishing on the frozen lake.

Three boat ramps serve the reservoir, one at Witcher Cove along the southeast shore, the other two on the north side near North Shore Campground. Boaters are advised to use caution, especially sailors, who are challenged by strong, tricky gusts of wind and fast-rising storms that

Directions:
From Colorado Springs, drive west on U.S. Highway 24 for 38 miles to Lake George. One mile west of Lake George, turn left on Park County Road 90 and follow it 10 miles to the park entrance.

Phone or write:
Eleven Mile State Park
Star Route 2, Box 4229
Lake George, Colorado 80827
(719) 748-3401

occasionally pass through the area. Boaters should be extra careful when they are within 150 feet of the rough, rocky shore.

At an elevation of 8,600 feet above sea level, the water is usually cold. Water-contact sports such as swimming, waterskiing, wading, and scuba diving are prohibited. Windsurfers must wear a full wet suit or dry suit.

At the southeast end of the reservoir near the dam, approximately 100 acres of water are closed to the public. This area is not leased to the Division of Parks and Outdoor Recreation and is often patrolled by local law enforcement.

Golden Gate Canyon State Park

Standing on the wooden deck at Panorama Point, it's easy to understand how Native Americans loved this land now called Golden Gate Canyon State Park. On a clear day, the point offers a majestic view of the snowcapped mountains of the Front Range, from Longs Peak southward across the Indian Peaks Wilderness Area and the Continental Divide to Mount Evans.

Some 300 years ago, only Native Americans were aware of the striking beauty and the abundance of game found along the Front Range. The Ute Indians controlled the mountains, while the Cheyenne and Arapahoe dominated the plains. The eastern foothills of the Front Range served as a buffer zone between the territory of the Utes and the plains Indians. The plains Indians often entered the foothills to hunt and to gather quartz for weapons and tools. Whenever they entered this buffer zone, a battle was sure to occur.

Relations between the Indians and European explorers and fur trappers were good during the early nineteenth century. The first white pioneers began settling the area in 1859 as gold fever swept across the land. That same year, a toll road was built through Golden Gate Canyon and into the southern quarter of the present park. This steep and rugged road carried thousands of fortune hunters to the gold fields of Central City and Black Hawk. Because of the enormous amounts of gold mined around these communities, the area was called "the richest square mile on earth." No precious metals were found in Golden Gate itself, but the densely wooded hills provided timber for the mines, towns, and railroads. The abundance of quartz found in the rolling hills was used for building and decorations.

In 1861 a shorter and easier road was built along the narrow walls of Clear Creek Canyon. This new road dramatically decreased the traffic on the Golden Gate road. By 1871 the railroad had pushed through Clear Creek Canyon to the mining towns, ending the Golden Gate toll road's tenure as a major route to the gold fields. However, the road continued as an access road for homesteaders, loggers, and hunters.

For the next several decades, most of the inhabitants of Golden Gate Canyon and environs made their living by farming and ranching. Other economic activities came and went, including logging, quartz mining, and even bootlegging. These eventually gave way to recreation. In June 1960 the state of Colorado purchased a 200-acre tract of land in Gilpin County that became the nucleus of today's Golden Gate State Park. The 10,000-acre complex ranges in elevation from 7,600 feet along Ralston Creek at the eastern park boundary to the 10,400-foot Tremont Mountain in the northwest section of the park. Located only sixteen miles northwest of Golden, Golden Gate has everything from open grassy meadows to rolling hills covered with ponderosa and lodgepole pine, Douglas fir, blue spruce, and stands of aspen. Scattered across the terrain are mammoth outcroppings of granite that rise from the forest floor into the clear blue sky. It also offers a multitude of activities for each visitor. Camping, fishing, hiking, nature study, and sightseeing are only a few of the many recreational opportunities available.

The visitor center is a good place to begin exploring Golden Gate. Built in 1968 and dedicated in 1969, the center is located just inside the southeast park entrance and is open daily, year-round. It features an ecological and historical display, a topographical map of the park, and photo displays of the local geology, flora, and fauna. Next to the center, a wooden deck extends over Show Pond, where visitors can observe and feed large rainbow trout.

Visitors to Golden Gate are reminded of the park's heritage. Many of its main features are named after previous landowners, or notorious events of the past. Frazer Meadow got its name from the Frazer family that homesteaded the area in the late 1800s. Reverend's Ridge was named for a preacher who lived in the vicinity; the chimney on his cabin bore a cross made of quartz, which marked him as the "Man of God." The appellations Ole' Barn Knoll and Red Barns come from historic structures that still exist. Bootleg Bottom was a notorious moonshine production center during the 1920s; Kriley Pond was named after William Kriley, the original owner of the property.

Golden Gate has several day-use areas located along the roads that traverse the park. From the visitor center, Ralston Creek Road follows

Golden Gate Canyon State Park. Kriley Pond is found along Golden Gate Canyon Road west of the visitor center.

Ralston Creek in a northeasterly direction through the eastern half of the park, passing five picnic areas and the Frazer Meadow trailhead. The Ralston Roost, Round the Bend, Bridge Creek, and Ranch Ponds picnic areas all have numerous tables and fire grills. Visitors will find the Red Barn group picnic area on the east side of the park. This facility provides a rustic setting for groups of up to 100 people.

Slough Pond and Kriley Pond are next to Golden Gate Canyon Road between the visitor center and the Mountain Base Road entrance station. These two man-made ponds create an ideal setting for children who are developing their fishing skills. A wooden deck on the south side of Kriley Pond has been designed for handicapped fishermen. Several picnic tables with fire grills surround the parking area.

Mountain Base Road parallels the western park boundary before reaching Reverend's Ridge in the northwest corner of the park. Along the way it passes Bootleg Bottom, Ole' Barn Knoll, and Kriley Pond Overlook, all of which have picnic sites and hiking trails. The Kriley Pond Overlook sits atop a knoll, providing visitors with a 360-degree view of the park. This fine sight still can't match the one at Panorama Point, which has to be the most visited area of Golden Gate. Located in

Golden Gate Canyon State Park. The most popular area of Golden Gate is Panorama Point. From here, visitors have a majestic view of the snowcapped mountains of the Front Range, from Longs Peak southward across the Indian Peaks Wilderness Area and the Continental Divide to Mount Evans.

the northwest corner of the park, it has a stunning vista. The late evening hours are the most colorful time of the day, as the burning sun casts a reddish glow across the snowcapped mountains. For many years this placid scene has created a romantic setting for spring and summer weddings.

Aside from its day-use areas, Golden Gate has three campgrounds that can accommodate tents, trailers, pickup campers, and motor homes. Reverend's Ridge Campground, located at the northwest corner of the park, consists of 106 campsites spread out over ten loops. Each campsite is equipped with a table and fire grill; flush toilets, showers, water hydrants, and a laundry are also provided. A dump station is located next to the Loop B entrance. On Friday and Saturday evenings each summer, park rangers and naturalists present campfire programs on a variety of outdoor topics at the adjacent amphitheater.

Aspen Meadows Campground is located in the north-central area of the park. Three areas — The Meadows, Twin Creek Loop, and Conifer

Loop — provide a total of twenty-six campsites for tents only. The Rimrock Loop has nine sites designed for horesback riders. (Horse campers may also ride to the remote Deer Creek campsites after first obtaining the necessary permit from the visitor center.) Facilities at Aspen Meadow include tables and grills at each site, with water hydrants and vault toilets nearby.

The Rifleman Phillips Group Campground, about a mile east of Aspen Meadow, is a tent-only campground for up to seventy-five people. Facilities include tables, fire grills, water hydrants, and vault toilets.

For people who want a more primitive camping experience, Golden Gate has twenty-three backcountry tent sites located at Frazer Meadow, Greenfield Meadow, Rim Meadow, Forgotten Valley, and along Deer Creek. Backcountry camping permits can be obtained on a first-come, first-served basis from the visitor center. Fires are not allowed in the backcountry, and there are no facilities available; campers are advised to bring a camping stove and an ample supply of water.

Backcountry explorers may also opt for the four backcountry shelters, three-sided structures with a roof and wooden floor built in the Appalachian trail-hut tradition. The shelters are ten by sixteen feet and can sleep six people comfortably. Strategically placed along the trail system, the huts have become a popular form of refuge for hikers and cross-country skiers and can be rented on a first-come, first-served basis.

Fishing for rainbow trout is permitted in any stream or pond (except Show Pond, next to the visitor center). Slough Pond, Kriley Pond, Dude's Fishing Hole, and the Ranch Ponds are periodically stocked by the Colorado Division of Wildlife. Limited hunting is allowed in the park during the regular hunting season. Hunting seasons change annually; for dates and regulations, contact the park office.

Hiking and nature study are the most popular activities at Golden Gate. There are three nature programs designed to challenge, entertain, and enlighten people of all ages.

The Adventure Pack Program offers activity packs that include identification guides for rocks, birds, and plants, study scopes, map and compass, pH test kits, and a variety of other items. They can be obtained free of charge at the visitor center or the Reverend's Ridge Campground office.

The Junior Ranger Program is for kids between the ages of six and twelve. They complete six of the program's activities and earn an official certificate. When they complete nine activities, they receive an official shoulder patch. Information on the Junior Ranger Program may be obtained at the visitor center or Reverend's Ridge Campground.

The most popular program for adults is the "I Hiked Golden Gate" program. In this program, visitors are rewarded for their hiking activities, receiving a pin for racking up 50 miles and another for hiking 100 miles. Those energetic souls who hike 150 miles have their names engraved on a plaque that hangs at the visitor center.

Nearly sixty miles of trails in the park offer a rewarding experience for hikers. Each of the fourteen trails is named for an animal native to the area and marked with the animal's footprint. The difficulty of the trail is indicated by the background shape and color of the trail marker. Of the sixty miles of trails, twenty-five are open to horses and twenty to mountain bikes. There are no stables at Golden Gate, but equestrians will find ample parking space for horse trailers at several trailhead parking areas found along the main roads in the park. Finally, about twenty miles of snowshoeing and cross-country skiing trails facilitate winter explorations of the park.

The Buffalo Trail is an easy 3.2-mile trail that begins at the Bridge Creek picnic area and ends at the Rifleman Phillips Group Campground. The trail passes by an old homestead in Forgotten Valley, as well as three primitive campsites and a backcountry shelter.

The easy Burro Trail begins at the Bridge Creek picnic area and ends 5.5 miles later at an old quarry that once yielded white quartz. Two trails branch off the main trail and travel north to Windy Peak. The first trail is short but steep; the second is longer but easier. The trail joins the Mountain Lion Trail for one stretch before turning north and ending at the old quarry. In the section of trail where the Mountain Lion Trail and the Burro Trail are joined, campers will find several primitive campsites and a backcountry shelter.

The Eagle Trail, an easy 2.1-mile path begins at Nott Creek and ends at City Lights Ridge. It follows the north side of Ralston Creek, goes west across the Burro and Buffalo Trails, and climbs the steep switchbacks to the top of City Lights Ridge. The summit commands a scenic view of Denver to the east and Forgotten Valley and Thorodin Mountain to the north.

The Elk Trail is an easy 2.2-mile trail that starts along Mountain Base Road and ends at Gap Hole. This trail passes through an open, flowery meadow next to an old homestead cabin, then continues northward along the west park boundary through a densely wooded area before crossing Gilpin County Road 2. The trail continues downhill, intersects the Raccoon Trail, and ends at Gap Hole.

The Horseshoe Trail, an easy 1.8-mile trail that begins at the Frazer Meadow trailhead and ends at Frazer Meadow, follows an old road up the valley through dense stands of pine and aspen before joining the Mule Deer Trail. Hikers will find an old homesteader's cabin in a scenic setting, with Frazer Meadow to the south and Tremont Mountain to the north.

The Mountain Lion Trail is an easy 6.0-mile trail. Starting at Nott Creek, it meanders through the northeast section of the park and ends at Forgotten Valley. For a short distance, the Mountain Lion Trail and the Burro Trail are united. Along this section of the trail, hikers will find three primitive campsites and a backcountry shelter. The trail continues along Deer Creek before climbing toward Windy Peak. At this point the trail divides; one branch joins the Burro Trail to the summit of Windy Peak, while the other extends into Forgotten Valley and meets the Buffalo Trail.

The Mule Deer Trail is an easy 4.7-mile hike from Lower Mountain Base Road to Panorama Point. Passing through the western half of the park, the Mule Deer Trail provides access to the Ground Squirrel, Blue Grouse, Horseshoe, and Coyote trails. Just past the Coyote Trail junction, the Mule Deer Trail passes by six primitive campsites and a backcountry shelter, then continues northward past the Aspen Meadow Campground to its terminus at Panorama Point.

The Ground Squirrel Trail, 2.3 miles long, begins at the Kriley Pond Overlook and passes through flower-filled Rim Meadow. The Blue Grouse Trail also starts at Kriley Pond and climbs a steep ridge before reaching Rim Meadow. There are five primitive campsites nestled in the aspens along Rim Meadow.

The Raccoon Trail is a moderate 3.5-mile trail beginning at Reverend's Ridge Campground. This route crosses the Elk Trail, climbs the steep hill to Panorama Point, and makes a large downhill loop to Gap Hole. From here the Raccoon Trail joins the Elk Trail for the return hike to the campgrounds.

Snowshoe Hare is another moderate trail. It forms a large 3-mile loop that begins at the Aspen Meadow Campground. The trail extends

Directions:
From the junction of Colorado Highway 58 and Interstate 70, follow Colorado 58 to a junction with U.S. Highway 6 and Colorado Highway 93 (Foothills Road). From this junction, drive north on Colorado 93 for 1.4 miles. Turn west on Golden Gate Canyon Road and follow it for 15 miles to the park entrance.

Phone or write:
Golden Gate Canyon State Park
3873 Highway 46
Golden, Colorado 80403
(303) 592-1502

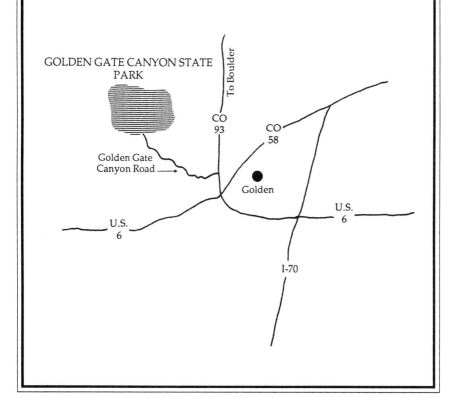

southward to Dude's Fishing Hole, continues southeast, then turns north to the Rifleman Phillips Group Campground before finally returning to the Aspen Meadow Campground.

The Black Bear Trail is a difficult 2.0-mile trail that starts at the Ralston Roost Trailhead east of the visitor's center. It meanders through numerous rock outcrops before meeting the Blue Grouse Trail on Ralston Roost.

The difficult 2.8-mile Blue Grouse Trail begins at the Kriley Pond Overlook, follows the same route as the Ground Squirrel Trail until it reaches a flattened ridge, turns south toward Ralston Roost, and drops down the steep hill past the Beaver Trail junction and Slough Pond.

The Coyote Trail is a beautiful but difficult 2.0-mile path that commences at the Bootleg Bottom picnic area. It climbs past an old cabin and a pavement roller that rumbled down the mountain during construction of Mountain Base Road. The route continues over Promontory Ridge and concludes when it joins the Mule Deer Trail at Frazer Meadow.

Finally, the Beaver Trail begins at the visitor center and makes a difficult 2.5-mile crossing southward across Golden Gate Canyon Road. It winds through a diversified habitat to the crest of a ridge from which hikers can view the Continental Divide. At the end of the trail lies the third backcountry shelter. This path forms a loop that returns to the road. From here, hikers can walk to Slough Pond or return to the visitors center.

A nominal fee purchases a small booklet called *The Trails of Golden Gate Canyon.* This pamphlet gives detailed descriptions of the trails, their flora and fauna, and a list of hiking tips to make the experience more enjoyable.

Harvey Gap State Park

During the summer of 1876, a small group of scientists known as the Hayden Survey Party was exploring and mapping the Cactus Valley and Silt Mesa. This narrow strip of land between the Grand River (now the Colorado River) and the Grand Hogback lies just north of the present-day town of Silt, Colorado. Dr. A. C. Peale, a geologist for the survey party reported that the Cactus Valley region was "hopelessly arid" and that unless some means of irrigation could be devised, the land would be useless. Only prickly pear cactus, yucca, greasewood, and sagebrush could survive in this desert.

At the north end of Cactus Valley, the party discovered a natural cut through the Grand Hogback. This opening allowed access to the open valley north of the ridge. The surveyors called the gap Hogback Pass.

Because the large meadow north of the hogback was home to a family of Ute Indians, it was dubbed Old Squaw's Camp after the old but energetic Indian woman who was the leading spirit of the family. The Utes lived in teepees and wickiups, giving up their nomadic lifestyle to inhabit the valley on a permanent basis. They owned roughly sixty head of cattle and a large herd of horses. From the opening in the hogback, they could view the scenic Cactus Valley below. Sadly, the Utes were expelled and placed on reservations after the Meeker massacre, an 1879 attack by Utes on white settlers in another part of the state. John Harvey claimed the vacated land north of Hogback Pass. Old Squaw's Camp became the Harvey Ranch, and the name Hogback Pass was changed to Harvey Gap.

Whites began to develop the resources of the region. The 1889 coal-mining boom brought hundreds of miners into the area. The remains of a once-productive coal mine are still visible along the steep

Harvey Gap State Park. Harvey Gap has developed the reputation of being a premier windsurfing area. The early morning hours are usually calm and quiet. By about 10 A.M., strong gusty winds blow in from Cactus Valley through Harvey Gap, creating a windsurfer's paradise.

Harvey Gap State Park. Aside from windsurfing, Harvey Gap is also noted for its fine fishing.

walls of Harvey Gap. Farming also began in earnest. Between 1887 and 1908, several businesses were set up to acquire property, secure water rights, and develop an irrigation system for the fruit orchards and ranchers in the valley. In 1891 the Grass Valley Land and Development Company began to build a dam across the natural gap in the hogback. At the same time, the Grass Valley Canal was being built. Beginning near Rifle Falls, the canal would transport water from East Rifle Creek to the reservoir. The dam was completed in 1894; local communities celebrated and dedicated the new structure that December.

But in the spring of 1895 the earthen dam broke, sending a wall of water through Harvey Gap and into Cactus Valley. Fortunately, there was no loss of human life, and personal property damage was minimal. Several ranchers did lose large numbers of livestock, and sections of the railroad tracks west of Silt were washed out. (Many of the large boulders that were swept down the gap are still visible at the base of the hogback.) With the aid of Japanese laborers, the Farmers Irrigation Company rebuilt the dam in 1903. In 1907 it was enlarged and strengthened to contain a larger reservoir.

Directions:
From the west side of Silt at the intersection of U.S. Highway 6 and First Street, drive north on First for 1.5 miles, then left on Garfield County Road 233 for about 1 mile. Drive north on Garfield County Road 237 (also known as Harvey Gap Road) through Harvey Gap to the park entrance.

Phone or write:
Harvey Gap State Park
c/o Rifle Gap State Park
0050 Road 219
Rifle, Colorado 81650
(303) 625-1607

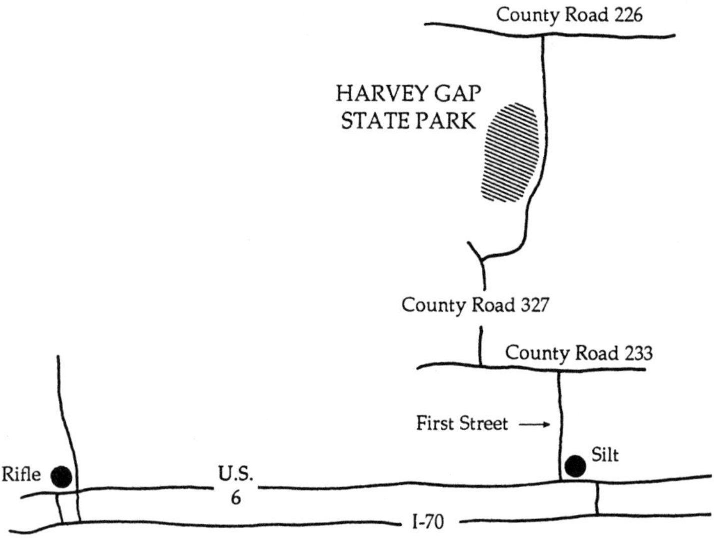

County Road 226

HARVEY GAP
STATE PARK

County Road 327

County Road 233

First Street →

Rifle ●   U.S.
6

Silt ●

I-70

Harvey Gap is now owned by the Farmers Irrigation Company and managed by the Silt Water Conservancy District. The recreational facilities of Harvey Gap State Park (formerly Harvey Gap State Recreation Area) have been managed by the Colorado Division of Parks and Outdoor Recreation since the fall of 1987. The 320-acre park is a day-use area with three recreational facilities located along the east shore. Each facility is accessible by following Garfield County Road 237, which parallels the east park boundary.

In the southeast corner of the lake, visitors will find a swim beach and picnic area sheltered by tall cottonwood trees. No lifeguards oversee the area, so individuals swim at their own risk. Perched atop a saddle just north of the swim beach is the Ridge picnic area. From the ridge, visitors are rewarded with a panoramic view of the lake and the Grand Hogback.

About a quarter-mile north of the Ridge picnic area lies Wind Surf Point. Harvey Gap has developed a reputation as a premiere windsurfing area. The early morning hours are usually calm and quiet. By about 10 A.M., strong gusty winds blow in from Cactus Valley through Harvey Gap, creating a windsurfer's paradise.

Aside from swimming and windsurfing, boating, scuba diving, and sailing are popular diversions at Harvey. Boats used on Harvey must have an engine of twenty horsepower or less. The one boat ramp that serves the lake is located north of the parking area at the main park entrance along the east shore. Several picnic tables with grills are scattered nearby.

Anglers enjoy fishing for bass, rainbow trout, catfish, sunfish, and crappie in the summer. During the winter ice fishing for trout can be an interesting experience.

Camping is not allowed at Harvey. However, there are numerous campsites at Rifle Gap and Rifle Falls six miles to the northwest.

Highline State Park

In prehistoric times, western Colorado was part of a vast tropical environment ruled by giant reptiles. Today, the Western Slope is dominated by desertlike plateaus. Located at the edge of the desert Southwest is a large, arid tract of land known as the Grand Valley. The valley floor consists of Mancos shale, a 4,000-foot-thick sedimentary layer that covers most of the region. The combination of shale and aridity reduced vegetation to predominantly sage and rabbitbrush.

The first settlers migrated into the valley in 1881. Prior to that time, only Native Americans ventured into this barren but beautiful landscape. Pioneers soon learned that the poor soil conditions and limited water would support few if any crops. However, the introduction of irrigation in the early 1900s changed the Grand Valley into a pleasant living environment. The state of Colorado authorized the building of the Highline Canal in 1891, but construction did not begin until 1912. The Highline Canal tunnel started in DeBeque Canyon just north of present-day Island Acres State Park and channeled water from the Grand River (now the Colorado River) beneath the Book Cliffs to the Grand Valley.

The abundance of water supplied by the canal raised the possibility of building a lake exclusively for recreation. The idea was presented to the governor and several cabinet members in Grand Junction in 1963. The proposed site was adjacent to Mack Mesa Lake, built in 1954 under a cooperative arrangement between the U.S. Fish and Wildlife Service and the Colorado Game and Fish Department. Because of land acquisition, development, and construction problems, the new Highline Lake did not become a reality until 1969.

Approximately twenty miles northwest of Grand Junction, Highline State Park (formerly Highline State Recreation Area) consists of 622 acres, including the 160-acre Highline Lake and the 14-acre Mack Mesa

Highline State Park. North Knoll above Mack Mesa Lake has become a unique nature study area. It is the only area in the park that supports nearly all the plant species found in the surrounding region. North Knoll contains at least nine species not found elsewhere in the park.

Lake. The park provides the only water-based public recreation facility in the Grand Valley. As a result, the park operates at capacity, especially on weekends, throughout the spring, summer, and early autumn.

Highline Lake provides good fishing, especially for catfish and crappie. Mack Mesa Lake has become noted for its trout fishing. On the southwest side of Mack Mesa Lake is a man-made jetty designed for handicapped fishermen. Meanwhile, the northern shore of Highline and the cattails lining the shore of Mack Mesa Lake have become a bird watcher's haven. Over 150 species of birds have been identified, including great blue heron, golden and bald eagles, white pelicans, pheasants, and snowy egrets. During the winter months, large numbers of migrating birds and waterfowl use the park as a resting area. Hunting at Highline is restricted to waterfowl during the regular hunting season.

The Grand Valley's plant life changed dramatically with the arrival of irrigation. A retired professor of botany, Jean Young, studied the area in 1983 and identified approximately 195 plant species within park boundaries. A copy of her report and a list of the plants she discovered are available for review at the park office. Also of interest to naturalists

Highline State Park. Visitors will find the swim beach to be a refreshing change. Instead of a sand beach, a manicured lawn extends from the picnic area down to the water's edge.

is the North Knoll above Mack Mesa Lake, which supports nearly all the plant species found in the surrounding Loma Hills. The knoll also contains at least nine species not found elsewhere in the park.

For visitors interested in paleontology, the Highline area is a dream come true. Although the park itself does not abound in fossils, the palisades that surround the valley are rich in the remains of prehistoric creatures. The Book Cliffs, only a few miles to the north, have yielded many fossils of prehistoric fish. To the south, along the Colorado River, are Dinosaur Hill and the Rabbit Valley Dinosaur Quarry, areas renowned for their rich deposits of fossil remains. In fact, dinosaur bones were discovered in the Grand Valley nine years before they were found in the now-famous Dinosaur National Monument some 140 miles to the north. In 1900 Dr. Elmer Riggs, curator of paleontology at the Field Museum of Natural History in Chicago, unearthed the world's first brachiosaurus and brontosaurus skeletons in two locations near Grand Junction.

Hunting for fossils fascinates many visitors, but water sports are the big attraction at Highline. The warm water provides a comfortable setting for boating, windsurfing, sailing, waterskiing, and swimming. While most of the recreational facilities are located at the southeast

Directions:
From Grand Junction, take Interstate 70 west to the Loma exit, go north on Colorado Highway 139 for 6 miles to Q Road, west 1.2 miles to 11.8 Road, then north 1 mile to the park entrance.

Phone or write:
Highline State Park
1800 11.8 Road
Loma, Colorado 81524
(303) 858-7208

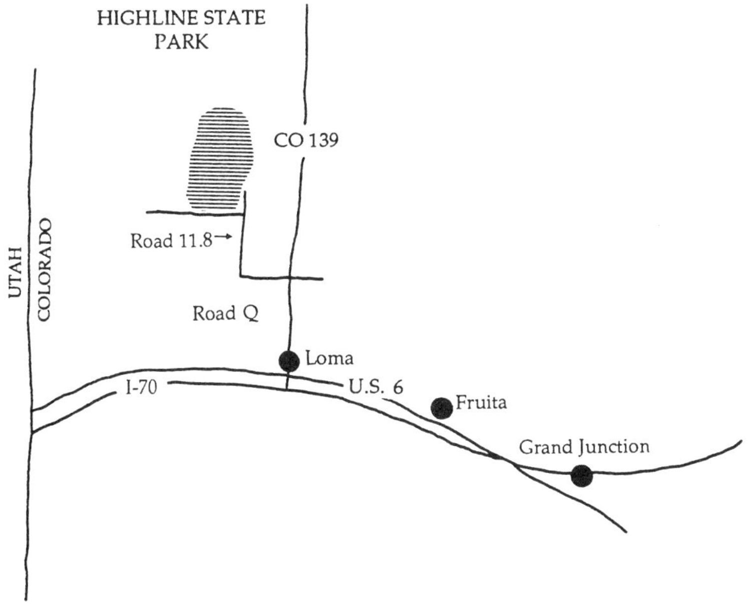

HIGHLINE STATE
PARK

CO 139

Road 11.8 →

UTAH

COLORADO

Road Q

Loma

I-70

U.S. 6

Fruita

Grand Junction

corner of the park, the boat ramp (with ample parking space) is found along the west shoreline. Visitors will find the swim beach to be a refreshing change: Instead of a sand beach, a manicured lawn extends from the picnic area down to the water's edge.

Mowed lawns also surround the camping and group picnic areas, which are shaded by tall cottonwoods, creating a relaxed, citylike atmosphere. The campground has twenty-five grassy campsites that can accommodate tents, trailers, and motor homes. Each site includes a table and grill with a vault toilet nearby. Flush toilets and water are available at the day-use area next to the campground. A dump station is located within the campground. There are no electrical hookups, but future plans include equipping the campground with full modern facilities.

Highline's administrators also plan to acquire land along the west boundary. The additional property will make it possible to build a nature center, extend hiking and bicycle trails around both lakes, and put in a new primitive campsite and several boat-in campsites.

Island Acres State Park

The geologic history of Colorado goes back more than 570 million years into the oldest division of geologic time, the Precambrian Era. During this early period, mountains grew skyward in Colorado and across the North American continent. Then, over the past 70 million years or so, the opposing forces of uplift and erosion sculpted the plateaus and canyons of the Western Slope. The powerful currents of the Colorado River carved out an 800-foot-deep gorge, leaving behind a large island. This same island can be found today only fifteen miles east of Grand Junction in the heart of DeBeque Canyon. It is now known as Island Acres State Park (formerly Island Acres State Recreation Area).

History reveals that this scenic area was once a favorite campsite and hunting ground for the Ute Indians, as well as trappers and explorers. From the early 1900s until 1967, it was called Island Ranch and used to raise peaches and livestock. In the 1950s a dike was built to irrigate local farms and create more grazing land. The dike eliminated the true island and altered the river to its present-day course. In December 1966 the Colorado Department of Highways purchased the property from Gus and Ruth Epeneter and used it to extract gravel for the construction of Interstate 70. The excavations created four water-filled pits, which were transformed into a state recreation area in 1967.

Sandwiched between the Colorado River on the west and Interstate 70 on the east, Island Acres is now a 139-acre park. Over 100,000 people visit the park annually, most of them residents of local communities, to enjoy picnicking, swimming, and year-round fishing. The park is also an attractive resting place for motorists traveling along I-70.

The four lakes do not have names — they are simply numbered 1 through 4. Lakes Number 1, 3, and 4 offer good fishing as they are stocked with trout by the Colorado Division of Wildlife. The west side of

Island Acres State Park. Of the four lakes at Island Acres, Lake Number 2 is reserved for swimming. A large sand beach circles half the lake.

Lake Number 1 has a concrete fishing pier providing safe, secure wheelchair access. Only nonmotorized boats such as kayaks, small rubber rafts, and canoes are permitted on the lakes.

Lake Number 2 is reserved for swimming. It features a large sand beach that circles half the lake. No official lifeguard is on duty, but during periods of peak usage (usually on summer weekends) a uniformed park ranger patrols the area on foot.

Many visitors are puzzled to find no canal, nor any other means to fill the lakes. Dick Fletcher, park manager of Island Acres, explains this phenomenon: "The lakes are filled by underground seepage from the Colorado River. The water level of the lakes is equal to the water level of the river. In May and June, when the river is high from the spring runoff, the water level rises in the lakes. In late summer, as the river recedes, the water in the lakes also recede."

The park offers a three-quarter-mile nature trail that follows the river bank. During the evening it is not unusual to observe mule deer, cottontail rabbits, blue herons, and bald eagles, all of which are common to the park and surrounding area. With a pair of binoculars, one can observe waterfowl nesting on several small islands in the middle of the

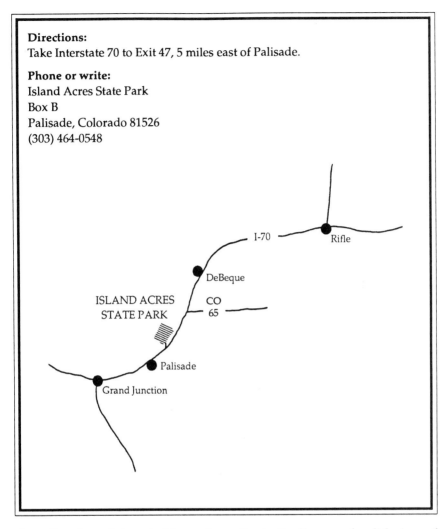

Directions:
Take Interstate 70 to Exit 47, 5 miles east of Palisade.

Phone or write:
Island Acres State Park
Box B
Palisade, Colorado 81526
(303) 464-0548

river. For those interested in geology, the trail offers a splendid view of the rugged palisades. The stunningly eroded cliffs reveal millions of years of the geologic past.

At the southeast corner of the park, visitors will find numerous picnic tables with grills. There are also several tables scattered around Lakes 1 and 2. Island Acres also has thirty-two grassy campsites that can accommodate tents, campers, and motor homes. Each site has a table and grill, with vault toilets and water hydrants nearby. Future plans include outfitting the campground with full facilities. A dump station is located between Lakes Number 3 and 4.

Jackson Lake State Park

Most people believe that the best recreation in Colorado is found in the mountains. They may be surprised to discover interesting destinations on the prairies east of Interstate 25. One of the most interesting is Jackson Lake State Park (formerly Jackson Lake State Recreation Area).

Jackson Lake is twenty-two miles northwest of Fort Morgan at approximately 4,400 feet above sea level. Local residents consider it an ocean on the prairie, a perfect place for water sports, fishing, and camping. The sandy lake bottom is free of obstructions, and beautiful beaches lined with tall cottonwood trees border the water.

The region along the South Platte River was originally inhabited by the nomadic Sioux, Cheyenne, and Arapahoe Indians. French explorers Peter and Paul Mallet are credited with naming the North and South Platte rivers. They probably chose the name because they used a *platte* (a flat-bottomed river boat) to navigate the river in 1739. Early explorers claimed the river to be "a mile wide and an inch thick" as it flowed across the Great Plains. Others joked that the muddy water was "too thick to drink, too thin to plow."

With the discovery of gold in the Rockies, the Overland Trail was developed along the South Platte into Denver. The new trail was heavily used by the Overland Stage Company, which carried thousands of pioneers to the Front Range. The Fifty-niners and their wagon trains also clung to the trail as they plodded across the barren plains. Today's Interstate 76 follows the same basic route across northeast Colorado as did the Overland Trail.

When Major Stephen H. Long explored the open territory of the prairie in 1820, he reported that the area was "almost wholly unfit for cultivation." With only the South Platte River as a water source, the land would be uninhabitable for people depending on agriculture. Long had

Jackson Lake State Park. Jackson's sandy beaches and gradually sloping lake bottom make for an ideal swimming area. There are two designated swim beaches. One lies along the west shore between the Cove and the Lakeside campgrounds; the second is found at the south shore.

no way of knowing that within 100 years, miles of irrigation canals and numerous reservoirs would be built to serve the agricultural needs of the arid plains.

Jackson Reservoir was built for water storage and irrigation purposes in 1901–1902 by the South Platte Land, Reservoir and Irrigation Company. The reservoir was named after B. W. Jackson, the secretary of the company. It is fed by a series of canals from the South Platte River beginning near the town of Masters. The land around the reservoir was used primarily for grazing until 1962, when the state began to purchase property around the lake for hunting and fishing. In 1965 the Colorado Game, Fish and Parks Department assumed responsibility for the recreational facilities. The park is now managed by the Division of Parks and Outdoor Recreation.

The recreational facilities at Jackson Lake are on the west and south shores. Between the two areas, in the southwest corner of the park, is Jackson Lake Village, a privately owned marina and trailer park. This is the only section of the park that is closed to the public.

Jackson Lake State Park. Jackson Lake is popular for its lakeside camping along the west shore.

The 2,700-acre lake is a haven for waterskiing, jet skiing, wind-surfing, and sailing enthusiasts. In addition, Jackson's sandy beaches and gradually sloping lake bottom make an ideal swimming area. There are two designated swim beaches, one along the west shore between the Cove and Lakeside campgrounds, the other at the south shore. When water is released in late summer for irrigation, the lake level falls and the beach areas increase in size. There are no lifeguards on duty, so individuals swim at their own risk. Children under twelve must be accompanied by an adult.

At the northern end of the west shore, a boat ramp extends approximately 750 feet into the lake. This ramp is large enough to be used as a fishing pier and is wheelchair accessible. The Jackson Lake Marina and a concession building stand next to the ramp. The concession provides boat rental and fuel, plus camping, fishing, and boating accessories. Food and beverages are also available. Another boat ramp can be found at the north shore day-use area. The north shore is considered a wildlife habitat area and is managed by the Colorado Division of Wildlife.

Jackson Lake has become known for its warm-water fishing. Anglers are delighted to find an abundance of yellow perch, catfish, walleye,

Directions:
From the intersection of Interstate 76 and Colorado Highway 39 just east of Wiggins, drive 7.25 miles north on Colorado 39 through Goodrich. Turn west on Morgan County Road Y5 and follow the paved road for 2.5 miles to the park entrance.

Phone or write:
Jackson Lake State Park
26363 County Road 3
Orchard, Colorado 80649
(303) 645-2551

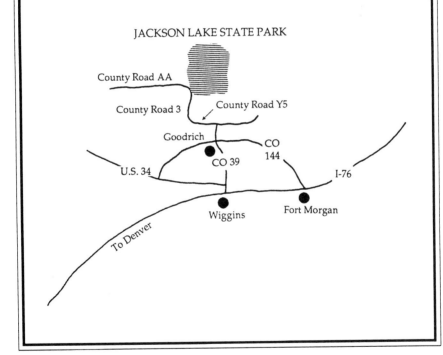

JACKSON LAKE STATE PARK

County Road AA

County Road 3   County Road Y5

Goodrich

CO 39   CO 144

U.S. 34   I-76

Wiggins   Fort Morgan

To Denver

bass, crappie, and rainbow trout, all of which are periodically stocked by the Division of Wildlife. Fishing is prohibited around the swim beaches and during the migratory waterfowl season.

Hunters come to Jackson for the plenitude of waterfowl, doves, pheasants, and rabbits. They must use bows and arrows or shotguns loaded with bird shot; waterfowl hunters must use steel shot. The regular hunting season begins on the Tuesday after Labor Day and ends on the Friday prior to Memorial Day.

Jackson provides two large day-use picnic sites. One, located near the concession building along the west shore, offers several sheltered tables, grills, a vault toilet, and a small fishing jetty. At the other picnic site, located along the south shore just east of the Loop B Campground, visitors will find numerous tables and grills shaded by tall cottonwood trees. Additional picnic tables can be found near the south shore entrance and scattered along the south shore.

Jackson Lake's five campgrounds contain 185 campsites for tents, trailers, pickup campers, and motor homes. The Pelican, Cove, and Lakeside campgrounds, all situated on the west shore, include tables, grills, and water hydrants at each site. At the Pelican and Lakeside campgrounds, campers can dock their boats next to their campsite. The Cove Campground has more modern facilities, namely flush toilets, showers, and an amphitheater where rangers provide interpretive programs on a variety of topics. These programs are held on Saturday evenings during the summer months.

The other two campgrounds are located on the south shore. The Loop A Campground provides sheltered tables with grills at each site, while the Loop B Campground provides unsheltered tables with grills. One restroom facility with flush toilets and showers serves both campgrounds. Electrical hookups are not available anywhere at Jackson Lake. A dump station is located near the west shore entrance.

Lake Pueblo State Park

What began as a typical spring day became a nightmare for the citizens of Pueblo and the surrounding area. On June 3, 1921, the clear blue skies over the Arkansas Valley were slowly darkened by a giant, stationary thunderstorm that dumped billions of gallons of water to the north and west of Pueblo. Records show that eleven inches of rain fell about twenty-five miles west of Pueblo on the town of Portland. By early evening, the usually calm Arkansas River and Foundation Creek joined to form a turbulent wall of water. An estimated 100,000 cubic feet of water per second raged through Pueblo. Residents could barely recognize their city the next morning. The water eroded the streets and swept trains off their tracks. Over 500 homes were destroyed, another 350 were condemned, and numerous businesses were washed away.

The cost of the flood was over $16 million — and this was in 1921! The loss of human life was even more devastating to the community. Over 150 people were killed, with another 142 unaccounted for. The skeletal remains of several victims were found thirty years after the flood.

It took many years for the area to rebuild. But over time Pueblo rebounded from the catastrophe. In March 1988, after a three-year study by the University of Kentucky, Pueblo County was ranked first out of 253 urban counties in terms of quality of life. The researchers focused on urban conditions, climate, and natural environment, basing their research on popular values rather than their own opinions. One factor contributing to the high quality of life in Pueblo County is Lake Pueblo State Park (formerly Lake Pueblo State Recreational Area). This 13,691-acre park's main attractions, the Pueblo Dam and Lake Pueblo, were built largely as a result of the horrendous flood of 1921. Soon after the

disaster, farmers, ranchers, and urban leaders began talking and express-
ing ideas on how to improve water storage and flood control. During the
late 1920s and through the 1930s, federal engineers studied the landscape for potential sites to build dams and levees. They continued talking through the 1940s, expanding the scope of their plans to include
diverting water from the Western Slope across the Continental Divide to
the Arkansas River. Ultimately, the vision for the Fryingpan-Arkansas
Project came to include transporting water from the Fryingpan River
over the divide to the Arkansas, providing hydroelectric power, supple-
mental irrigation, municipal and industrial water, recreation, conservation, development of wildlife habitat, and flood control.

In January 1955 the chambers of commerce in Pueblo, La Junta,
Cañon City, and Salida declared Water Week to promote the project.
Chamber members sold frying pans in an effort to raise money to send
backers of the project to Washington, D.C. Burros carried the frying pans
to towns in the valley. Small pans sold for $5 and large ones for $100 or
more. By the end of the week, over $30,000 had been raised.

The project faced stiff opposition on Colorado's Western Slope and
in several western states. Representative J. Edgar Chenoweth led the
fight for the project in the House of Representatives through the 1950s.
After many years of debate, the House approved the Fryingpan-Arkansas Project on June 13, 1962. The Senate followed suit on August 6, 1962.
President John F. Kennedy signed the project into law on August 16; the
following day he flew to Pueblo to tour the site. Roughly 12,000 people
filled the stands of the Pueblo Public Schools football stadium as Senator
John Carroll, Governor Stephen McNichols and U.S. Secretary of the
Interior Stewart Udall presented President Kennedy with a souvenir
frying pan.

President Kennedy's speech lasted for about fifteen minutes. He
told the crowd, "This project is an investment in the future of the country and the growth of the West. I hope this project will write a conservation record second to none. This is a great country. I believe it deserves
the best for its citizens."

Construction of the Fryingpan-Arkansas Project began in 1964. The
U.S. Bureau of Reclamation purchased 360 acres of land east of Basalt to
build the 285-foot-high earth-filled Ruedi Dam on the Fryingpan River,
completing it in 1968. Construction of the Divide Tunnel — renamed the
Boustead Tunnel in honor of Charles H. Boustead, the first general

manager of the Southern Colorado Water Conservancy District — began in 1966. It took six years to complete the 5.4-mile-long passageway. With a diameter of 10.5 feet, the tunnel conveys 120,000 acre-feet of water annually from Ruedi Reservoir beneath the Continental Divide into Turquoise Lake, which was expanded in 1968.

From Turquoise Lake, water is transported nearly eleven miles via the Mount Elbert Conduit to the Mount Elbert Power Plant at Twin Lakes. The lakes originally formed when a glacial moraine dammed Lake Creek. Both construction of the power plant and the enlargement of Twin Lakes began in 1971 and were completed in 1981. This pumped storage power plant, with its two 138,000-horsepower hydroelectric turbine generators, can produce 200 megawatts of electrical power. The plant operates only for peak power needs rather than continuously.

From Twin Lakes, water flows into the Arkansas River, where it drops roughly 4,000 feet in elevation in the 150-mile journey to Lake Pueblo. Ground was broken for the Pueblo Dam on August 26, 1967. Two years later, the concrete "plug" that forms the base of the dam was completed. Construction on the dam itself began in 1970 and was finished in 1975. The massive dam is 200 feet high and 10,500 feet in length, 60 feet short of two miles. Two components were later added to the system. In 1985, the Fountain Valley Pipeline was opened to transport water from Lake Pueblo to the Colorado Springs area, thirty-five miles to the north. And the final phase of the Fryingpan-Arkansas Project, the Pueblo Fish Hatchery below Pueblo Dam, was built between 1986 and September 1990. Managed by the Colorado Division of Wildlife, the hatchery produces seven species of fish that will eventually stock lakes and streams throughout Colorado.

As the dam was being built, large tracts of land were reserved for recreation, fishing, and wildlife habitat. The Bureau of Reclamation, in conjunction with the National Park Service and the Colorado Division of Parks and Outdoor Recreation, developed a master plan to build recreational facilities at Lake Pueblo. This ultramodern park was divided into four large recreation areas: Arkansas Point, Rock Canyon, Juniper Breaks, and the Northern Plains.

A visit to Lake Pueblo begins at the visitor center at Arkansas Point, which sits on an upland plain in the southeast corner of the park. The center provides several large photo displays and maps that illustrate the history, geology, and wildlife of the park. There is also an auditorium

Lake Pueblo State Park. The major attractions at the Rock Canyon day-use area are the large swimming lake and sand beach. Rock Canyon lies east of Pueblo Dam between the Arkansas River and Anticline Ridge.

where park rangers and naturalists give interpretive outdoor programs every week.

A new campground is currently under construction at Arkansas Point. When completed, the campground will offer 111 new campsites, four of them designed to accommodate handicapped guests. Each campsite will have sheltered tables with grills and electrical hookups; additional facilities will include flush toilets, showers, and a fish-cleaning station.

The second recreation area, Rock Canyon, is located in the riparian zone of the Arkansas River between the dam and the limestone cliffs of Anticline Ridge. This day-use facility is by far the largest and most modern in the state park system. Visitors are often amazed at the variety of recreational opportunities available to them.

The big attractions are the natural lake and the large beach that circles it. Sunbathers come here to soak up the warm Colorado rays. A pavilion provides locker rooms, showers, a first-aid station, and a food concession. Behind the beach is a grassy belt with several picnic sites, a volleyball field, and a children's playground. Perhaps the busiest place at Rock Canyon is the giant waterslide just west of the beach. On a hot summer day, hundreds of people splash down the triple slide into a cool, refreshing pool. An adjacent concession building rents paddleboats and bumper boats and sells food and beverages. This day-use facility is open daily during the summer months from 11:00 A.M. to 7:00 P.M. However, the beach and picnic facilities can be reserved for after-hours use. A nominal fee is charged to enter the swimming area.

South of the swimming area is Anticline Lake, more commonly known as the fishing pond. This small lake is periodically stocked with trout, bass, bluegill, and bullhead. On the south end of the pond, a wooden deck extends over the lake. This wheelchair-accessible platform provides safe, secure fishing for handicapped anglers. Physical fitness buffs can make use of the quarter-mile Paracourse fitness circuit that circles Anticline Lake. The eighteen exercise stations were designed on the research conducted in cooperation with the physiologists and sports medicine experts of the National Athletic Health Institute.

Several picnic areas complete the picture at Rock Canyon. The Red Tail and Marsh Hawk picnic sites are found between the swimming area and the fishing pond. The Osprey is located in the southeast corner of Rock Canyon next to the river. On the south side of the river lie the Cottonwood Grove and the Snakeskin picnic sites. There is also a group site for up to 100 people. Each picnic site is equipped with tables, grills, a volleyball court, and a playground. Juniper Breaks, the third recreation area, lies along the jagged north shore between the marina and the dam. This area is currently under construction; when completed, it will offer a modern campground, a primitive walk-in campground, and numerous picnic sites.

The fourth recreation facility, Northern Plains, is located in the northwest section of the park on an open plain. Northern Plains has everything outdoor enthusiasts could ask for. There are three camp-grounds, including a large group campground with three loops. The Prairie Ridge and Yucca Flats campgrounds both have paved pull-through and back-in sites for tents, trailers, pickup campers, and large motor homes. Each site has a sheltered table, grill, and electrical hookup. Additional facilities include flush toilets, showers, water hydrants, fish-cleaning stations, soft drink machines, and several children's play-grounds. Both Prairie Ridge and Yucca Flats have dump stations next to the entrance, as well as four sites designed for handicapped campers. Kettle Creek, the third campground, has forty primitive campsites, each with a table, grill, and nearby vault toilets and water hydrants.

Just north of the campgrounds, visitors will find the uniquely designed Lake Pueblo amphitheater, where rangers present nature programs. The amphitheater also serves as a "nature calendar." Its east wall has several large pillars resembling the giant stones at Stonehenge in England. Looking eastward from a point on the stage, one can locate the rising point of the sun on the first day of each season by sighting a post on the horizon through the center slot on the theater wall. The amphitheater also has a sundial that can be used to measure local time during daylight hours and a Polaris pointer to locate the North Star. Early sea captains and explorers used similar tools to locate Polaris during their journeys. There are also two group picnic areas at Northern Plains. Each site is sheltered and can accommodate up to 120 people. And next to the north entrance station is an airplane field for radio-controlled model planes. Currently there are no local flying clubs utilizing this airstrip. However, the airfield is open to the public.

Fishing and water sports are the big attractions at Lake Pueblo. The 4,646-acre lake is periodically stocked with catfish, crappie, sunfish, walleye, wipers, and rainbow and brown trout. Black bass also inhabit these waters; however, any bass under fifteen inches long must be returned. Several fishing access areas dot the shoreline.

Lake Pueblo's warm water makes it ideal for waterskiing, jet skiing, windsurfing, and sailing. In the southeast corner of the lake, below the visitor center, is a water ski take-off/drop-off area. Windsurfers enjoy a separate launch site along the northeast shore.

There are two marinas at Lake Pueblo. The South Shore Marina and boat ramp are located just west of the east entrance station. The North Shore Marina and boat ramp lie in a cove between Northern Plains and Juniper Breaks. This privately owned marina is the largest in the state park system. Both marinas offer boat and slip rental, fuel, camping and fishing accessories, and food and beverages.

Boaters should watch for debris and shallow areas that are a potential hazard to boats. As the water level decreases, standing underwater trees protrude above or just below the water level. Boaters are advised to check with park officials before entering this area, just west of the North Shore Marina.

Lake Pueblo State Park. The North Shore Marina lies in a cove between the Northern Plains and Juniper Breaks recreation areas. This privately owned concession is the largest marina in the state park system. It offers boat and slip rental, boat repair, fuel, and fishing and camping accessories. Food and beverages are also available.

Bicyclists, walkers, and joggers share the sixteen-mile paved Dam Trail that connects the various recreational areas. Beginning near the South Shore Marina at Arkansas Point, the trail extends down into Rock Canyon before continuing around to the North Shore Marina. From the Rock Canyon area, the Dam Trail intersects the Pueblo River Trail, which leads into the city of Pueblo. Another path, the Overlook Trail, begins near the campground at Arkansas Point and goes to the top of a jagged ridge with several buttes that tower over the park. From the summit, visitors enjoy a colorful view of the reservoir and the snowcapped Pikes Peak to the north.

In addition to possessing a wealth of recreational opportunities, Lake Pueblo is ideal for people interested in geology and nature study. This semidesert area evolved through three major geologic periods, beginning with the Cretaceous some 70 million years ago. At that time, southern Colorado was buried by a tropical ocean, and calcium sediments were deposited on the ocean floor. These sediments — horizontal

Lake Pueblo State Park. The horizontal layers of sedimentary sandstone, shale, and lime-stone are visible on the upland slopes and cliffs formed during the Cretaceous Period some seventy million years ago. At that time southern Colorado was buried by a sea, and calcium sediments were deposited on the ocean floor.

layers of sandstone, shale, and limestone — are still visible in the upland slopes and cliffs. The next geologic period was marked by volcanic uplift and faulting, exposing saw-toothed layers of the earth's crust; an example is the Rock Canyon Anticline parallel to the eastern park boundary. In the final period, the Arkansas River and its tributaries eroded the previously deposited sediments. It was during this time that the irregular limestone cliffs and buttes on Lake Pueblo's shore were formed.

Visitors who take the time to explore the cliffs often uncover ancient fossils. They commonly find peelecypods (clams), palmoxylon (petrified palm tree trunks), and inoceramus (a giant thick-shelled creature that had a shell an inch thick and was roughly three feet long). Keep in mind that the Antiquities Act of 1906 prohibits the removal of natural elements such as fossils, plants, or wildlife from any state or national park. Study the ancient remains, but leave them so others may also enjoy them.

The western edge of the park is a wildlife management area administered by the Division of Wildlife. An abundance of animals can be

114

Directions:
From the intersection of Interstate 25 and U.S. Highway 50, go west on U.S. 50 for 4 miles, then head south on Pueblo Boulevard for 4 miles. Turn west on Thatcher Boulevard and drive 6 miles to the east gate entrance. From Pueblo West, go south on McCulloch Boulevard for 3.7 miles, turn south on Nichols Road and follow it to the north entrance.

Phone or write:
Lake Pueblo State Park
640 Pueblo Reservoir Road
Pueblo, Colorado 81005
(719) 561-9320
North Shore Marina: (719) 547-3880
South Shore Marina: (719) 561-1043
Ranger Station/Campground: (719) 547-2343
Rock Canyon Swim Beach: (719) 564-0065

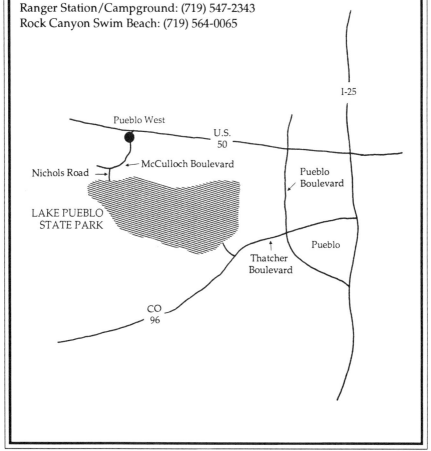

observed and photographed in this area, including mule and white-tailed deer, coyotes, rabbits, prairie dogs, and badgers. Birds also seek refuge at Lake Pueblo, most notably wild turkeys, eagles, great blue herons, roadrunners, and a variety of waterfowl.

In recent years, two uncommon plant species have been found on rock outcrops in the Arkansas Valley and within the park boundaries. The round-leaf four-o-clock and the dwarf milkweed are rare, and their habitat is limited. These plants have been listed in *Rare Plants of Colorado*, a book published by the Nature Plant Society.

Lathrop State Park

The Spanish Conquistadors ventured into New Mexico and Colorado in the seventeenth century with the motto "Gold, Glory, and Gospel." By 1680 they had enslaved the Native Americans in New Mexico and imposed harsh taxes. Many of the Indians fled north into Colorado to a site called Cuartelejo, roughly a hundred miles east of today's Pueblo. When the Spanish came to retrieve the refugees, the open plains between Pueblo and Walsenburg witnessed numerous battles.

The Comanches acquired rifles from the French in the 1700s and became increasingly hostile toward the Spanish. They killed sheepherders, soldiers, and missionaries and raided small communities, killing the men and capturing women and children. In 1778 Juan Bautista de Anza, founder of San Francisco, was appointed governor of New Mexico. He led a vigorous campaign with 600 Spanish troops into what is now Colorado, intending to teach the Comanches and their leader, Chief Greenhorn, a severe lesson. Aided by several Ute and Arapahoe braves, Anza soundly defeated the Comanches in seven battles and killed the chief at the base of Greenhorn Mountain along Greenhorn Creek, both of which were named after the dead warrior. After this fierce fighting, peace was established with the Indians.

Greenhorn Mountain and the site of this famous battle are about twenty miles north of today's Lathrop State Park. The park lies on the high plains of the Cucharas Valley only three miles west of Walsenburg. Lathrop became Colorado's first state park (as opposed to a state recreation area) in 1962. It was named after Harold W. Lathrop, the first director of the state parks and recreation board from 1957 until his death in August 1961.

Lathrop is a 1,050-acre park with two reservoirs, Martin and Horseshoe lakes, that account for 320 acres between them. They were built for irrigation purposes by farmers and ranchers in 1909. Originally, Martin Lake was called Oehm Lake and Horseshoe Lake was called Meriam Lake. The names were changed in 1941 when the city of Walsenburg purchased the water rights. The city expanded the lakes to provide Walsenburg with an ample supply of water. They are fed by the Coler Ditch, which transports water from the Cucharas River to the Walsenburg Reservoir southwest of the park. From there, water is channeled into Horseshoe Lake and then into Martin Lake.

A good place to begin a visit to Lathrop is the visitor center next to the park entrance. Twelve large murals painted by Paul Busch decorate the interior walls. These paintings portray the history of Colorado from the era of the Mesa Verde cliff dwellers to the coal miner strikes of the 1920s. The center also has several display panels that identify plants and animals found throughout the area.

People that come to Lathrop are always fascinated by the two massive mountains to the southwest that rise abruptly from the valley floor. These are the Spanish Peaks: East Spanish Peak at 12,669 feet and West Spanish Peak at 13,610 feet above sea level. These mountains were formed 30 million years ago when masses of molten lava pushed up into layers of sedimentary rock. In time the softer sedimentary layers eroded away, exposing the hard, resistant rock of the peaks.

The Pueblo Indians called the mountains *Huajatolla* (Wa-ha-toy-a), meaning "breasts of the earth." Native people believed that all life originated in these mountains, strange, mysterious places inhabited by gods of lost tribes. According to Indian legend, no one standing in the shadows of the peaks would die, and all dreams of a person sleeping near them would come true. Another legend claimed that the mountains contained an abundance of gold, which the Indians used as an offering to the gods. Then three Spanish priests arrived in the area meaning to bring religion to the Indians. However, one of the priests was corrupt. He forced the men to mine the sacred gold, then killed them and fled to Mexico, a destination he never reached. Somewhere along the way he vanished. Years later, in 1811, large nuggets of gold were found on the desert plains, miles from any natural gold source.

The most popular place at Lathrop on a hot summer day is the beach on the south shore of Martin Lake. The beach includes a take-off/drop-off area for water-skiers. A boat ramp serving Martin Lake is also located along the south shore. Windsurfers enjoy a separate beach and picnic area at Windsurfer Cove along the north shore.

Lathrop State Park. An attractive feature at Lathrop is the nine-hole golf course. The course is owned by the state but is managed by the city of Walsenburg and Huerfano County.

Several fishing access and picnic areas are scattered around Martin Lake: the North and South Inlet areas on the west side, Rock Outcrop and Huajatolla Cove along the north shore, Golfball Cove in the northeast section, and the West Beach picnic area in the northwest corner of the lake. This last area offers several sheltered sites with tables and grills. An additional fishing area on the east side is a concrete dike for disabled sportsmen.

Horseshoe Lake offers sailing, boating at wakeless speed (under ten miles per hour), fishing, and windsurfing. The boat ramp that serves Horseshoe Lake is located at the southeast corner. Several unnamed fishing access areas dot the west and north shores. The hunting of waterfowl and small game is permitted only at the posted areas around Horseshoe Lake. Only shotguns and bows and arrows are allowed, and only during the regular hunting season.

Both lakes are stocked periodically with rainbow trout, channel catfish, bass, bluegill, and crappie. Martin Lake is also stocked with walleye and wipers, while Horseshoe Lake features tiger muskie.

In addition to water sports, Lathrop offers good opportunities for hiking. The 1.75-mile Hogback Ridge Trail begins from a small parking

Directions:
Go 3 miles west of Walsenburg on U.S. Highway 160 and turn north into park entrance.

Phone or write:
Lathrop State Park
70 County Road 502
Walsenburg, Colorado 81089
(719) 738-2376
Golf course: (719) 738-2730

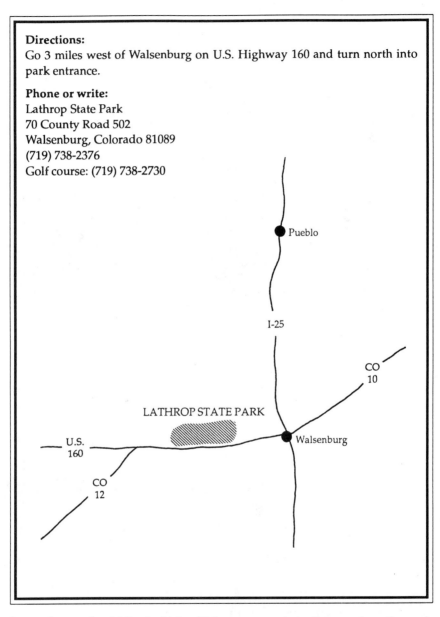

Pueblo

I-25

CO
10

LATHROP STATE PARK

U.S.
160

Walsenburg

CO
12

lot to the north of Martin Lake. This easy, scenic trail meanders through piñon pine and juniper, both common in southern Colorado. Hikers should stay on the trail, to avoid stepping on yucca and prickly pear cactus. The sharp spines of these plants have caused many a painful experience.

The trail passes into a field of massive sandstone boulders. The tops of these huge rocks have potholes spread across their flat surfaces. These holes are formed by rain and melting snow, which dissolve binding minerals and loosen sand granules. Winter freezing also contributes to this process. After many years, the loosened sand is blown and washed away, leaving a depression in the surface. Most of these holes are only a few inches deep. However, some of the older ones are twelve to fourteen inches deep. Potholes can contain mosses and transient communities of animal life that have evolved brief life cycles, some only hours long. A cycle begins when rainwater is retained in the depressions during warm weather. Larvae and eggs that have lain dormant and dehydrated in the pothole sediments for months, perhaps years, suddenly spring to life. The hatchlings rush through their growth and reproductive stages, leaving the next generations drying in the sediments before the water evaporates.

The trail concludes at the top of the hogback, yielding a spectacular 360-degree view. To the east is the endless shortgrass prairie; to the south and southwest, the Spanish Peaks and the Culebra Range of the Sangre de Cristo Mountains; to the west, Mount Maestas, and to the north, the Wet Mountains and Greenhorn Mountain.

Lathrop is adjacent to a nine-hole golf course with a pro shop and restaurant. The golf course is owned by the state but managed by the city of Walsenburg and Huerfano County. It stays open all year, weather permitting. The combination of fishing and golf attracts thousands of visitors from Texas, Kansas, and New Mexico each year.

Lathrop has two campgrounds with a total of ninety-eight campsites. The Yucca Campground, considered a primitive camping area, has nineteen sites and two group campsites. Each campsite has a table and grill with water hydrants and a vault toilet nearby. The Piñon Campground has seventy-nine paved pull-through sites with tables and grills; thirty-nine of these have electrical hookups. This modern campground provides flush toilets, a shower house, laundry, water hydrants, and a playground. Both campgrounds are equipped with dump stations.

Between the Piñon Campground and the rugged hogback is the park amphitheater. From Memorial Day through Labor Day on Friday and Saturday evenings, park rangers and naturalists provide slide lecture programs featuring the geology, history, and wildlife of the park and surrounding area.

Lory State Park

Lory State Park lies in an ecotone, a place of transition between two major ecosystems — the plains and the mountains, in this case. What make Lory unique are its unusual geologic formations, terrain, and vegetation, which change with altitude. The landscape progresses from the shortgrass prairie at 5,540 feet to the mountain shrub community and finally to the ponderosa pine forest 7,015 feet above sea level. With its diversity of ecosystems and abundance of wildlife, along with its potential for educational and recreational use, this pristine area was destined to become a state park, a place people come for hiking, picnicking, horseback riding, studying nature, or just relaxing.

In 1891 John Kimmons homesteaded a 160-acre tract of land beneath an outcrop called Arthur's Rock south of Bellvue. At the same time, John Howard homesteaded an area in North Park near Gould. In 1897 the two men traded ranches. Howard slowly built his new ranch into a 3,600-acre spread that he operated for sixty-five years.

Howard sold the land in the early 1960s, and in 1967 the Colorado Game, Fish and Parks Department purchased 2,352 acres of his old ranch. In 1976 the Colorado Division of Parks and Outdoor Recreation obtained and additional 140 acres.

Lory State Park was originally called Horsetooth State Recreation Area. However, this name caused considerable confusion because it was west of Horsetooth Reservoir and north of Horsetooth Mountain Park. To eliminate the confusion, the park's name was changed on October 17, 1975, in honor of Dr. Charles A. Lory, president of Colorado State University from 1909 to 1940.

The park is a geologic showcase that enables visitors to compare the three major rock types — sedimentary, metamorphic, and igneous — and how they have influenced each other over the past two billion years

Lory State Park. The geologic structure of Lory supports a large variety of plants. Mosses and these alpine saxifrage thrive in the moist rocky areas.

of mountain building. The hogback and the jagged coves of Horsetooth Reservoir along the eastern edge of the park consist of sedimentary rock from the Fountain Formation. Layers of red sandstone filled with iron compounds were created as streams deposited sand and gravel from the ancestral Rockies some 300 million years ago.

The oldest rocks at Lory are the metamorphic and igneous rocks concentrated in the western two-thirds of the park. Metamorphic rocks include quartz, semischist, calcium silicate, amphibolites, and gneisses, all approximately 1.75 billion years old. Arthur's Rock, the park's most prominent feature at 6,780 feet, is made of igneous rock, a resistant granite pegmatite estimated to be 1.7 billion years old.

The geologic structure of Lory supports a large diversity of plants, including three distinct plant communities, creating a unique mixture of prairie and mountain species. Vegetation patterns throughout the foothills are influenced by topography, soils, and moisture.

The grassland community is in the flatter, lower elevations of the park in the plains life zone. Soils are relatively deep and rich, the climate dry and warm. Plants in this community have adapted by developing deep root systems. Cheatgrass is the most dominant species, along with needle-and-thread grass and blue grama grass. Prickly poppy, rabbit-brush, yucca, and prickly pear cactus are scattered across the landscape.

The brushland community is found in the valleys and rocky hill-sides of the foothills life zone. The shallow, rocky soil erodes easily during heavy rains. Mountain mahogany and skunkbrush thrive along the rugged slopes. The pasque flower, the first wildflower to bloom in spring, adds a touch of color. During the late spring and summer months, harebells, bluebells, Indian paintbrush, and wild geranium swing with the gentle breeze.

The ponderosa pine community is found in the highest elevations of the park in the lower montane life zone. This area of the park receives the most rainfall during the summer months. Because the water table in this zone is deep under the ground, plants growing in the community have evolved long taproots. Ponderosa pine is the most common tree here. These trees naturally space themselves to ensure that each gets an adequate supply of moisture.

All three communities contain riparian zones that lie adjacent to the small, intermittently flowing streams and springs in the park. These creeks support a variety of plants, including willows, cottonwoods, ferns, alders, chokecherry, and lichens. Lory is also home to several plants listed as species of special concern by the Colorado Natural Areas program. The wood lily, which is rare in Colorado, can be found on the high ridges the ponderosa pine community. The Rocky Mountain spikemoss, a fernlike plant, grows on the north-facing cliffs of the brush-land and ponderosa pine communities.

Lory has as much diversity in wildlife as in vegetation. Creatures range in size from millipedes to mule deer. Butterflies skip and dance throughout the park. Each summer members of the local Xerces Society (an international nonprofit group dedicated to the conservation of rare invertebrates and their habitats) study and count the butterflies. They have found that over 100 species of butterflies pass through or breed at Lory. Careful observers can also find the rare Calico grasshopper in the tall grasses throughout the park.

At least eight species of reptiles live at Lory, including the red-lipped prairie lizard and the prairie-lined race runner. Six species of snakes have been identified, the most common being the bull snake and the prairie rattlesnake. Rattlesnakes generally shy away from people but can be dangerous if they feel threatened. Birds are abundant at Lory, too. In 1988 a publication titled *Lory State Park and Horsetooth County Park*

Bird List identified 177 bird species that inhabit the area. Some of the most common are the western meadowlark, magpie, mourning dove, canyon wren, and western tanager. Golden eagles are often visible around the high wooded ridges. Although waterfowl and shorebirds are not common in the park itself, they can be observed along the eastern boundary near neighboring Horsetooth Reservoir.

Lory's mammal population is large and prosperous. Mule deer thrive at Lory, feeding on the abundant mountain mahogany. Raccoons, Albert's squirrels, coyotes, skunks, and porcupines are commonly seen throughout the park. In the more remote sections of Lory, black bear, bobcats, and mountain lions are occasionally sighted within the park boundaries.

In an effort to preserve the natural environment of this 2,492-acre sanctuary, park management has limited road access into Lory to one thoroughfare that runs parallel to the east boundary. Along this road at the north end of the park, visitors will find the sheltered Timber Trail group picnic area, which has tables, barbecue grills, horseshoe pits, and a volleyball court. This site can accommodate up to 120 people and can be reserved in advance.

The Eltuck picnic area has five sheltered tables surrounded by a large grassy lawn, making it popular for weddings and family reunions. At the Old Homestead picnic area, the original site of the John Kimmons homestead, there are numerous individual picnic tables with fire grills. Several are shaded by trees remaining from the old homestead. Individual picnic tables can also be found at the south end of the park near the Arthur's Rock trailhead.

Lory is a premier equestrian area. The Double Diamond Stables in the northeast corner of the park offer guided breakfast rides, dinner rides, hay rides, and sleigh rides for children and adults. At the southern tip of the park is a 320-acre cross-country jumping course. Each spring, the Northern Colorado chapter of the Mountain States Combined Training Association sponsors a cross-country competition. Over 100 riders of all ages come from Colorado, Wyoming, Nebraska, Montana, and New Mexico to enter this prestigious event.

Furthermore, the rangers at Lory State Park have been assisted by the Northern Colorado Mounted Patrol of the Rockies since 1986. Members of this volunteer organization patrol the park on horseback to promote good relations between different user groups, provide the general public with information about the park, and enforce public safety.

Each member completes a training period before being accepted into the patrol, receiving instruction in park rules and regulations, public relations, map reading, first aid and CPR, trail etiquette and safety, and horsemanship.

Without a doubt, hiking is the most popular activity at Lory. The park has eight named trails of varying difficulty that provide roughly twenty-five miles of scenic pleasure. Some of the routes are abandoned logging and ranch roads; several short trails extend from the main road down to Eltuck Bay and Orchard Cove on Horsetooth Reservoir. Many of the routes are open to horseback riders, joggers, and mountain bikers. There are no facilities available, so trail users must bring their own water supply.

The Waterfall Trail begins at the Timber Trail picnic area. This leisurely tenth-of-a-mile walk leads to a series of small waterfalls active in the spring and early summer. This trail was built by Boy Scout Troop 82 in 1981. The Timber Trail also begins at the Timber Trail picnic area. The 3.5-mile path is open to hiking, mountain biking, and horseback riding. It starts in the grassland plant community, passes through the shrub community, and enters the ponderosa pine forest, where it intersects with the Well Gulch Trail and provides access to Arthur's Rock.

Six primitive backcountry campsites are located along the Timber Trail; permits are available at the park entrance station. Open fires are not permitted in the backcountry, so campers should bring a stove for cooking. Fresh water is available at the entrance station.

The Well Gulch and Howard Loop trails combine to create a self-guided nature trail. The Well Gulch Trail begins at the Eltuck picnic area, and ends at the Timber Trail. The Howard Loop route goes from the Old Homestead picnic area through the grassland community before joining the Well Gulch Trail. Twenty interpretive stations along the way illustrate the flora and fauna of the park. A brochure explaining these twenty stations can be obtained at the trailheads.

The Arthur's Rock Trail begins as two trails that join below Arthur's Rock. The foot trail begins at the parking lot and meanders 1.7 miles up through a narrow ravine before joining the horse trail, which starts next to the head of the Shoreline Trail. The horse route passes through the cross-country jumping area before meeting the foot trail and also provides access to Horsetooth Mountain Park, south of Lory. Both trails provide access to the summit of Arthur's Rock, which commands a majestic view of Horsetooth Reservoir and the city of Fort Collins.

Directions:
From Fort Collins, take U.S. Highway 287 north through LaPorte. At the Bellvue exit (Larimer County Road 52E) turn left and drive 1 mile to Larimer County Road 23N. Turn left and drive 1.4 miles to Larimer County Road 25G; turn right and go 1.6 miles to the park entrance.

Phone or write:
Lory State Park
708 Lodgepole Drive
Bellvue, Colorado 80512
(303) 493-1623
Double Diamond Stables: (303) 224-4200

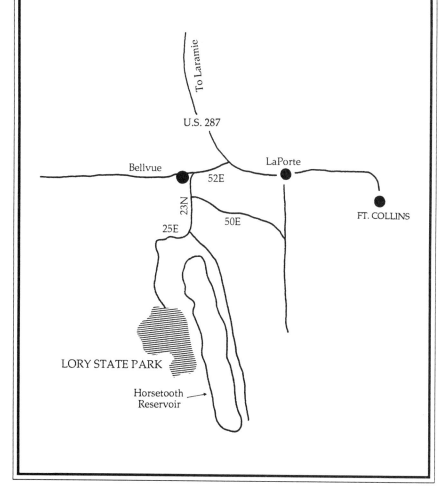

The Overlook Trail connects the Howard Loop and Arthur's Rock trails. Approximately 1.9 miles in length, it gives hikers the chance to view a variety of vegetative habitats and an abundance of wildlife. Finally, the mile-long Shoreline Trail begins at the end of the park road, just north of the cross-country jumping area, and stretches through the red sandstone hogbacks to the shoreline of Horsetooth Reservoir.

Mancos State Park

It was not until the late 1770s that Europeans became aware of the beautiful Mancos Valley. In 1776 Franciscan fathers Francisco Atanasio Dominguez and Silvestre Velez de Escalante led an expedition of ten explorers from Santa Fe, a journey now known as the Dominguez-Escalante Expedition. Their purpose was to establish a route between Santa Fe, which was part of the declining Spanish empire, to Monterey, California, a Spanish presidio and the cultural center of the Pacific Coast. Passing through the southwest corner of present-day Colorado, they found snowcapped mountains and free-flowing rivers. The explorers named a river that ran through a large open valley *Rio de los Mancos*, which means "the river of the cripple," after one of the expedition members was injured.

White people began to settle this arid valley nearly one hundred years later, in 1874. In 1881 the town of Mancos was laid out, making it the oldest town in today's Montezuma County. A Quaker family named Wetherill that emigrated from Pennsylvania owned a ranch in the valley called Alamo Ranch. In 1888 Richard Wetherill and his brother-in-law Charles Mason discovered the famous Anasazi ruin known as Cliff Palace and several other ruins while searching for stray cattle. For several years the Wetherill family escorted visitors by horseback into the rugged canyons to view the Anasazi remains. As the sites became popular, they were rapidly explored and ransacked. Baron Gustaf Nordenskiold, a Swedish scientist, was the first to perform scientific studies on the dwellings. During the exploration he sent a large quantity of artifacts back to Sweden.

After Nordenskiold explored the area, and after years of looting, Congress passed the Antiquities Act of 1906 to protect archaeological remains and artifacts. The National Park Service and the citizens of the

Mancos Valley wanted further protection for these unique dwellings, so in 1909 the rugged canyons and mesas that were once home to the Anasazi became Mesa Verde National Park.

Anasazi is a Navajo word meaning "ancient ones." These early natives were agricultural people who inhabited the Four Corners area from about A.D. 1 to A.D. 1300 It seems hard to believe, but the region supported a larger population a thousand years ago than it does today. Archaeologists are still puzzled by the sudden exodus of the Anasazi. We may never know the complete story of their existence, because they had no written records and many of their artifacts and buildings were destroyed. Many believe that the present-day Pueblo Indians of New Mexico and Arizona are their decendents.

The Anasazi's former homeland is now the home of Mancos State Park (formerly Mancos State Recreation Area). Located at the northern end of the Mancos Valley in a pristine setting at 7,800 feet above sea level, Mancos is surrounded by the San Juan National Forest to the north, the rugged La Plata Mountains to the east, and the great desert to the southwest. The 338-acre park's central feature, Jackson Gulch Dam and Reservoir, was built between 1941 and 1948 by the Bureau of Reclamation. The dam is managed by the Mancos Water Conservancy District. A canal diverts water from the West Mancos River into the 216-acre lake, which supplies drinking water for the town of Mancos and Mesa Verde National Park. The recreational facilities were built in the 1970s by the Young Adult Conservation Corps and are now managed by the Colorado Division of Parks and Outdoor Recreation. To avoid confusion, the division named the new park Mancos instead of Jackson Gulch because there already was a Jackson Lake on the plains northwest of Fort Morgan.

The big attraction at Mancos is the peace and quiet. Visitors can enjoy excellent fishing in a slow, relaxed atmosphere. Trout fishing is especially popular, as the lake is periodically stocked by the Colorado Division of Wildlife. For cold-weather enthusiasts, ice fishing and cross-country skiing are fun activities.

Mancos is well prepared for campers. The main campground along the lake's south side has twenty-four campsites sheltered by a mature ponderosa pine forest. Each site is equipped with a table and grill. A vault toilet, water hydrant, and dump station are available, but there are no electrical hookups. Nine additional campsites sit along the north shore. These sites are considered primitive and are primarily for tents. However, some of the sites are accessible to pickup campers and small

Directions:
From the town of Mancos, go north on Colorado Highway 184 for about a fourth of a mile and turn east on Montezuma County Road 42 (Forest Service Road 561). Go 4 miles to Montezuma County Road N, then turn west and follow it to the park entrance.

Phone or write:
Mancos State Park
c/o Navajo State Park
Box 1697
Arboles, Colorado 81121
(303) 883-2208

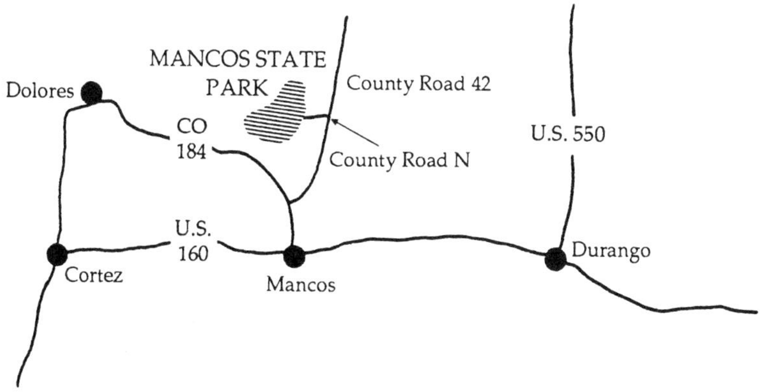

motor homes. Grills, tables, and vault toilets are available, but drinking water is not.

A number of activities are restricted. Boating at Mancos is limited to wakeless boating (under ten miles per hour). There is one boat ramp at the southeast corner of the lake next to the dam. Waterskiing and swimming are not permitted. Although hunting is not allowed within park boundaries, the park is often used as a base camp for big-game hunters during the regular hunting season.

A 3.5-mile trail (about half of which is West Side Road) circles the lake, giving hikers a scenic walk. Another path in the northwest area of the park extends 1.25 miles to the Chicken Creek Trail, which meanders eight miles through San Juan National Forest to the Transfer Campground (a forest service facility).

On the south side of the park next to the entrance station is a sheltered group picnic area. This day-use facility provides a volleyball field and a horseshoe pit. Along the north shore, visitors will find several more picnic sites nestled in the tall ponderosa pines.

Arkansas Headwaters Recreation Area. Whitewater rafting is the big attraction along the Arkansas River. There is more whitewater rafting on the Arkansas than any other river in the United States.

Barbour Ponds State Park. Sunrise over Barbour Ponds. Located in the shadow of Longs Peak, these man-made ponds were created when the Colorado Department of Highways used the land to extract gravel for the construction of Interstate 25.

Barr Lake State Park. Located approximately thirty miles northeast of Denver, the 2,600 acre Barr Lake State Park has become a wildlife sanctuary. The shore is lined with stands of cottonwood trees, marshes, and aquatic plants, which provide food and shelter for waterfowl and nongame birds.

Bonny State Park. Autumn is the most colorful time of year on the open Colorado prairie. Stands of cottonwood trees surrounding Bonny Reservoir add a splash of color to a semiarid region.

Boyd Lake State Park. Surrounded by farmland and residential areas, Boyd Lake has become a water sports haven for northern Colorado.

Castlewood Canyon State Park. On the northern slope of the Palmer Divide, Cherry Creek slices its way through the heart of Castlewood Canyon. Only thirty miles south of Denver, Castlewood Canyon is a unique environment with plants and trees that are more commonly found in the mountains than on the plains.

138

Chatfield State Park. In the southwest corner of the Denver metro area, the 5,378-acre Chatfield State Park has approximately thirty outdoor activities, something for every member of the family. More than 1.5 million visitors are attracted to the park each year.

Cherry Creek State Park. In the southeast corner of the Denver metro area, thousands of businesses and homes encircle Cherry Creek Reservoir. It's hard to believe that this popular recreation area was once part of the famous Smoky Hill Trail, which carried early pioneers on their westward journey.

Colorado State Forest State Park. Reflections of the 12,485 foot Nokhu Crags in Ranger Lakes, just south of Colorado Highway 14.

Crawford State Park. Crawford Reservoir lies in a narrow basin with the West Elk Mountains to the east and the Gunnison Uplift to the west. The latter feature continually rises upward to the rim of the Black Canyon of the Gunnison. The most notable landmark in the vicinity is Needle Rock, which lies to the northeast of the park.

140

Eldorado Canyon State Park. The jagged walls of Eldorado Canyon provide technical rock climbers with some of the most challenging routes found in the United States. There are over 500 routes, attracting climbers from almost every continent.

Eleven Mile State Park. Eleven Mile Reservoir is a 3,405-acre lake that provides approximately twenty-four miles of scenic shoreline.

Golden Gate Canyon State Park. The Horseshoe Trail ends at Frazer Meadow near this old homesteader's cabin, which lies in a scenic setting below 10,400-foot Tremont Mountain.

Harvey Gap State Park. Prior to the construction of the reservoir, this open meadow north of the Grand Hogback was home to a family of Ute Indians. The natural gap in the ridge was named Hogback Pass.

Highline State Park. Approximately twenty miles northwest of Grand Junction, Highline State Park is an oasis on the edge of the desert Southwest. The park provides the only water-based public recreation area in the Grand Valley.

Island Acres State Park. Reflections of the 800-foot sandstone walls of DeBeque Canyon. The ponds at Island Acres were created when the Colorado Department of Highways extracted gravel from the area to build Interstate 70. The small lakes are fed by underground seepage from the Colorado River.

Jackson Lake State Park. Many residents of northeastern Colorado claim that Jackson Lake is an ocean on the prairie. The sandy lake bottom is free of obstructions, and beautiful sand beaches lined with tall cottonwood trees border the water.

146

Lake Pueblo State Park. In March 1988, after a three-year study by the University of Kentucky, Pueblo County was ranked first out of 253 urban counties in terms of quality of life. The recreational opportunities at Lake Pueblo State Park contribute to Pueblo's high quality of life.

Lathrop State Park. Lathrop State Park lies on the high plains of the Cucharas Valley west of Walsenburg. Lathrop became Colorado's first state park (as opposed to state recreation area) in 1962.

Lory State Park. Equestrian cross-country jumping is a continuation of English tradition. Each spring, Lory State Park is host to a cross-country competition sponsored by the Northern Colorado chapter of the Mountain States Combined Training Association.

148

Mancos State Park. The big attraction at Mancos State Park is the peace and quiet. Visitors can enjoy great fishing in a slow, relaxed atmosphere.

Mueller State Park. At 9,047 feet above sea level, the massive Dome Rock is the most dominant formation within the park boundary.

Navajo State Park. The thirty-seven-mile-long Navajo Lake is a paradise for recreationists who enjoy unlimited space for boating, sailing, and fishing.

Paonia State Park. Located only sixteen miles east of the town of Paonia, the Paonia Dam and Reservoir was the first venture of the Colorado River Storage Project.

Pearl Lake State Park. The solitude and tranquility of Pearl Lake is truly one of Colorado's best kept secrets. Nestled in a pristine mountain setting, the lake is silent except for the gentle whispering of the wind through the pines.

Picnic Rock River Access Area. The Cache la Poudre River is the first stream on the Front Range to be protected under the National Wild and Scenic Rivers Act. Under this designation, seventy-five miles of the Poudre and its tributaries are preserved for future generations.

Ridgway State Park. Ridgway Reservoir is nearly five miles long and roughly a mile wide. Surrounded by 14,000-foot mountains, it has some of the most picturesque scenery in Colorado. Mount Sneffels and the San Juan Mountains lie to the south, with the Cimarron Mountains to the east and the Uncompahgre Plateau to the northwest.

Rifle Falls State Park. East Rifle Creek flows over a limestone cliff, creating a misty spray that drenches the grass and moss-covered rocks below. This placid, almost tropical paradise in an arid region has affectionately been named "Colorado's Hawaii."

Rifle Gap State Park. On the northern slope of the Grand Hogback just north of Rifle Gap is the 1,305-acre Rifle Gap State Park. With fishing, water sports, and camping as the major attractions, the park is truly a place for all outdoor enthusiasts.

Roxborough State Park. Because of its unique geology and diverse ecosystem, Roxborough became the first state park to be designated as a Colorado Natural Area in 1979 and as a National Natural Landmark in 1980. Unlike its cousins, Red Rocks to the north and Garden of the Gods to the south, Roxborough has no graffiti or roads to disturb the placid beauty.

Spinney Mountain State Park. The open hills and flat ground surrounding Spinney Mountain Reservoir resemble a shortgrass prairie.

Stagecoach State Park. Sunrise over Stagecoach State Park. Stagecoach lies in a scenic sagebrush basin the Ute Indians called *Egeria*, meaning "crooked woman," after the winding course of the Yampa River through the valley.

Steamboat Lake State Park. Steamboat Lake is a true paradise that lies in the broad basin between the picturesque Hahns Peak to the east and Sand Mountain to the west. Pine-covered hills with stands of aspen create colorful vistas around an open meadow.

Sweitzer Lake State Park. After a spring thunderstorm on the desertlike terrain, the sun bursts through the clouds, creating a colorful display of light over Sweitzer Lake.

161

Sylvan Lake State Park. Many people like to visit Sylvan in September to celebrate the turning of the aspen. As the days grow shorter and cooler temperatures prevail, the pale green aspen leaves turn bright yellow, creating patches of gold in a conifer forest. The vivid yellow and green hues against the red sandstone cliffs create an unforgettable scene.

162

Trinidad Lake State Park. By driving across Trinidad Dam, visitors are rewarded with a spectacular view of the lake and the Culebra Range of the Sangre de Cristo Mountains to the west.

Vega State Park. In late spring and early summer, the meadows surrounding Vega Lake become a sea of wildflowers. A colorful array of mules-ears, Indian paintbrush, and a variety of other flowers adds a splash of color to the lush green valley.

Mueller State Park

"Just look at that view! Isn't it marvelous? Wonderful!" These were the words uttered by President Theodore Roosevelt as he passed through the area west of Colorado Springs in 1901. Part of the majestic landscape that Roosevelt saw is now Mueller State Park and Wildlife Area. Lying at the western base of Pikes Peak, Mueller has a varied topography ranging from open grassy meadows to rolling hills covered with spruce, fir, pine, and stands of aspen. Scattered across the terrain are dramatic outcroppings of Pikes Peak granite that rise from the forest floor and protrude into the deep blue sky.

Mueller is the natural habitat of an abundance of wildlife. Large herds of elk, mule deer, and numerous smaller mammals are often observed throughout the park. In the more remote areas, black bears, bobcats, and an occasional mountain lion can roam free without human interference. A small herd of bighorn sheep resides in the park, while the larger Pikes Peak herd migrates annually into the park's Fourmile Creek area for winter shelter and spring lambing.

This region of Colorado once teemed with game, making it a favorite hunting ground for the Ute Indians. But in the early 1860s, thousands of prospectors and fortune hunters raced through the area to reach the goldfields of Cripple Creek and Victor. As the mining industry slowly petered out, the lush meadows were homesteaded and used for cattle ranching. Over the years, W. E. Mueller acquired several former ranches and homesteads and added them to his own Mueller Ranch. He believed in wildlife preservation and encouraged the Colorado Division of Wildlife to use his ranch for bighorn research. It was at Mueller Ranch that wildlife biologists found a way to control lungworm, a deadly parasite that was destroying large numbers of bighorn sheep.

By the 1970s rapid economic development had begun to encroach

Bighorn sheep are abundant at Mueller. A small herd resides in the park, while the large Pikes Peak herd migrates annually into the Fourmile Creek area for winter shelter and spring lambing.

upon the Mueller Ranch. Concerned about losing a natural wildlife refuge, the Division of Wildlife began negotiations with the Mueller family to purchase the property. The state could not raise enough capital to purchase the land, but in 1978 the Nature Conservancy bought the land for $5.2 million. That organization resold the property to the state of Colorado, which used funds from the state lottery and various donations to pay for the land.

Today, this 12,103-acre park is divided into three sections. The northern half is owned by the Colorado Division of Parks and Outdoor Recreation. The southern half, which is referred to as the Dome Rock Wildlife Area, is owned by the Division of Wildlife and jointly administered with the Division of Parks and Outdoor Recreation. In the southwest corner of the park is the 640-acre Dome Rock Natural Area, which is managed by the Division of Wildlife. Visitors enjoy year-round recreation, including camping, picnicking, hiking, and fishing. During the winter months, ice skating and cross-country skiing are popular. Regardless of the season, the scenic beauty and the abundance of wildlife create a nature lover's paradise.

Mueller State Park. The white trunks of these aspen trees are heavily scarred. This results from elk feeding on the tree bark during winter, when snow has buried the natural grasses. If the elk-chewed scars completely encircle the trunk, the tree usually dies.

Wapiti Road, the main artery through the park's high-use area, winds its way up to the summit of Revenuer's Ridge. The stands of aspen trees near the junction of Wapiti Road and Mountain Lion Road have heavily scarred trunks, the result of elk feeding on the bark during winter when heavy snow has buried the natural grasses. If the scars completely encircle the trunk, the tree usually dies.

Five scenic picnic areas provide forty-one individual picnic sites along Wapiti Road. They are Lost Pond, Bootlegger, Outlook, Rock Pond, and Preacher's Hollow. Each site is equipped with a table and grill with a water hydrant and vault toilet nearby. Wapiti Road continues along Revenuer's Ridge through a modern campground that offers ninety campsites, including twelve walk-in tent sites and a group camping area. The campground can accommodate tents, trailers, pickup campers, and motor homes. Each campsite has a table and fire grill. Electrical hookups are available at each site, with the exception of the walk-in tent sites. Additional facilities include flush toilets, showers, laundry, water hydrants, and a dump station near the campground entrance.

Plans are in the works to build a livery stable, a country store, and a concession for ski and bicycle rental. A new visitor center will be erected on a scenic overlook; when completed, it will have a variety of educational and informative displays on the history, wildlife, and geology of the park. There will also be ranger-led hikes and group presentations.

Mueller has over eighty-five miles of hiking on fifty-three interconnecting trails that invite visitors to explore the natural and historical features of the park. The trails are named and numbered and vary from short leisurely walks to full-day hikes. All trails are open to hiking. Some are used only for hiking and bicycling, while other trails are open only to hiking and horseback riding. Several trails are open to all three activities. A detailed map and trail guide is available at the park entrance gate.

Nine of the trails begin from the recreational sites on Revenuer's Ridge. Each eventually connects with one of the other fifty-three routes in the park. These nine trails extend downhill into the park, making for an easy and comfortable hike; but the return trip is uphill and could be strenuous.

The southern half of the park, Dome Rock Wildlife Area, can be reached by driving south of the main entrance on Colorado Highway 67 for 1.4 miles, then turning right on Teller County Road 61 for two miles to the wildlife area gate. This primitive area has no facilities of any kind. It does have the trailhead for the Dome Rock Trail, number 46. This

Directions:
Drive 25 miles west of Colorado Springs on U.S. Highway 24 to Divide. Turn south on Colorado Highway 67 and drive 3.8 miles, then turn right into the park entrance.

Phone or write:
Mueller State Park
Box 49
Divide, Colorado 80814
(719) 687-2366

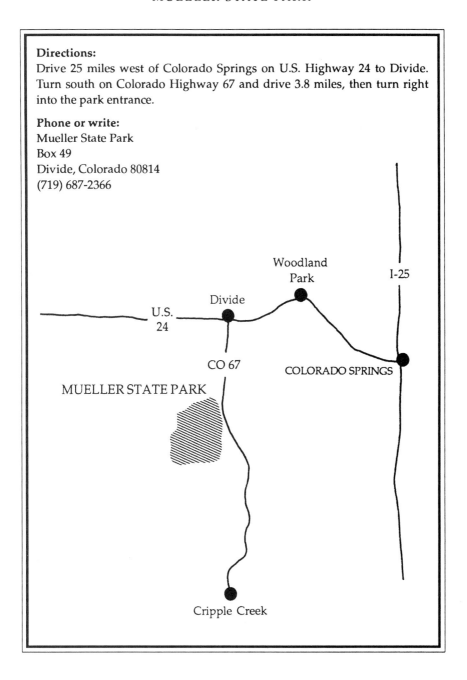

four-mile trail (one way) follows an old wagon road that parallels Fourmile Creek and crosses it on several occasions. The trail passes the old Sand Burr gold mine (which never provided an ounce of precious metal), then meanders beneath several towering rock formations, including the 9,577-foot Sheep Nose. At about the halfway point is the site of the historic Jackrabbit Lodge. Only the chimney remains of the once-posh hunting resort. The trail ends at a junction with the Spring Creek Trail, number 47, at the base of Dome Rock.

At 9,047 feet, the massive Dome Rock is the most prominent rock formation in the park. People who are not willing to endure an eight-mile hike but still want to see Dome Rock can view it from Teller County Road 1, about ten miles south of Florissant.

The 640-acre natural area encompassing Dome Rock is closed to the public from December 15 through May 15. This is a winter feeding ground and spring lambing area for bighorn sheep, which are protected by the Division of Wildlife.

Fishing is a popular attraction at Mueller. Anglers can fish for trout in Fourmile Creek, Werley Pond, Rock Pond, and Brook Pond. The Division of Wildlife periodically stocks these ponds with cutthroat and brook trout. Limited hunting is also permitted at Mueller. Information regarding the hunting seasons is available at the park headquarters.

Navajo State Park

The piñon-covered hills of southern Colorado and northern New Mexico were once the homeland of the Anasazi. Ancient spear points, surface and cave dwellings, and several gravesites indicate man lived along the San Juan and Piedra rivers for hundreds of years. Archaeologists have unearthed bits of pottery and the ruins of shallow pit houses that indicate that an agricultural life existed as early as A.D. 400 to A.D. 700. During that period the Anasazi developed simple pottery and surface dwellings built with upright poles and mud. Over the next several hundred years, they improved their farming techniques and masonry construction. For reasons still unknown to modern archaeologists, the ancient people abandoned the region around A.D. 1050. The most logical explanation for the exodus is severe drought and erosion of their fields.

It was not until the fourteenth century that the nomadic Ute and Navajo tribes settled along the San Juan River. Remnants of their pottery and their *pueblitos,* small masonry dwellings built in defensive locations for protection against raids by other tribes, are found throughout the valley.

The ten explorers of the Dominguez-Escalante Expedition were among the first white men to come to this region, passing through the Arboles, Colorado, area in 1776. The purpose of the expedition was to establish a route between Santa Fe, New Mexico, and Monterey, California. As European settlers began to migrate into the area, the Indians were slowly forced out of their land and onto reservations. Farmers and ranchers quickly seized the territory. Then, in the early 1880s, the Denver and Rio Grande Western Railroad pushed its tracks into this new frontier.

The railroad served the area until 1967 and became an important part of the economy, transporting agricultural produce from the farms to population centers. Farming was the backbone of the economy. Several irrigation ditches built from the San Juan River supplied farmers with an adequate water supply.

This area remains unpolluted and sparsely populated today. Located outside Arboles, roughly thirty-five miles southwest of Pagosa Springs, is Navajo State Park (formerly Navajo State Recreation Area). The big attraction, Navajo Lake, extends twenty-three miles from the Colorado state border to the dam. The distance between where the San Juan River enters the lake in Colorado and where the Pine River enters the lake in New Mexico is thirty-seven miles.

Construction of the Navajo Dam over the San Juan River began in July 1958. Built by the U.S. Bureau of Reclamation, the dam is roughly three-fourths of a mile long and 400 feet high. It was dedicated September 15, 1962.

Navajo Lake is one of the major reservoirs of the Colorado River Storage Project and the principal storage reservoir for the extensive Navajo Indian Irrigation Project. The latter will eventually irrigate about 110,000 acres of land on the Navajo Indian Reservation. Construction of the project was started in 1963 and the first water was delivered in 1976. This system, run entirely by Indians, was designed and is being built by the U.S. Bureau of Reclamation for the U.S. Bureau of Indian Affairs. As segments are completed, they are turned over to the Navajo tribe for operation and maintenance.

During the construction of the dam, fifty families had to relocate as private land was purchased for the reservoir. The small town of Rosa, New Mexico, about two miles south of the Colorado border, was inundated. Rosa was the most prosperous of the area's Hispanic settlements. During the Prohibition years of the 1920s, the village achieved a degree of notoriety by selling bootleg whiskey to drinkers in Durango. In its heyday, Rosa had a general store, a dance hall, an adobe church, and a cemetery and was considered the trade center for Hispanic settlements in the area. But the Great Depression brought a decline to the once-proud community.

Old Arboles was the only Colorado village lost due to the reservoir. Located between Archuleta County Road 500 and the confluence of the Piedra and San Juan Rivers, Old Arboles once served the area with a railroad station, post office, and general store. The post office was relocated to its present location near Colorado Highway 151.

Navajo became a state park in 1964 and is managed by the Colorado Division of Parks and Outdoor Recreation. The park comprises

Navajo State Park. Next to the visitor center parking lot is a large boulder with numerous petroglyphs carved on the surface. Among the figures depicted are three *yeis* (ceremonial godlike figures), a deer, a corn plant, and a horseback rider.

1,949 land acres and 3,000 surface acres of water. The Colorado Division of Wildlife manages the 520-acre Sambrito State Wildlife Area on the west side of the park.

The section of Navajo Lake in Colorado looks similar to the upper half of the letter *y*, with the Piedra River flowing in from the north and the San Juan River entering from the east. The lake is a paradise for recreationists who enjoy unlimited space for boating and fishing. Of Navajo's four developed recreation areas, three are in New Mexico: The Pine River, Sims Mesa, and San Juan River sites are all located near the dam.

The fourth recreation facility at Navajo is located in Colorado in the southwest corner of Navajo State Park. The park office and visitor center feature exhibits of Indian artifacts excavated from areas now submerged beneath the reservoir. There are also several displays that illustrate the history, geology, and wildlife of the region. Next to the visitor center parking lot is a large boulder with numerous petroglyphs carved on the surface. This particular rock was found along the Piedra River. Among the figures depicted are three *yeis* (ceremonial godlike figures), a deer, a

Navajo State Park. Near Wind Surf Beach, visitors can study two old freight cars and this water tower, which were once used by the railroad.

corn plant, and a horseback rider. Many cliffs around the reservoir contain petroglyphs believed to be of Navajo origin.

Boating is a favorite pastime at Navajo. The San Juan Marina is open from March through November. The marina, located about a quarter-mile west of the visitor center, provides boat and slip rental, fuel, and boat repair. A concession building provides food, beverages, and fishing and camping supplies. One of the unique features of the marina is the water-ski school at Mooring Cove, which offers lessons to beginners and advanced techniques for veteran skiers.

Below the marina sits what park rangers claim to be the longest boat ramp in Colorado: It is eighty feet wide and a quarter-mile long. Boaters must obey Colorado boating statues and regulations, which are available at the park entrance station. New Mexico laws and regulations apply to craft that cross the state line. The two states have a reciprocal agreement to honor each other's boat registrations and inspection stickers.

Overnight campers are welcome at Navajo. The campground has two large loops with seventy campsites for tents, trailers, pickup campers, and motor homes. Each site has a table and grill, with flush toilets

Navajo State Park. A houseboat is an excellent way to enjoy the great fishing available at Navajo Lake.

and a shower house nearby. A dump station is located within the campground. Between the campground and the marina, a large picnic area offers several individual sites and a group picnic site that can accommodate up to 100 people.

Navajo has a 3,100-foot-long grass/dirt airstrip, so visitors can fly into the park. Actually, the southern tip of the runway is in New Mexico. Nine tie-downs are provided to anchor grounded planes in gusty winds. No additional fee is charged for using this facility.

The two hiking trails at Navajo offer scenic views of the lake and surrounding hills. The Lake View Trail starts near the visitor center and extends half a mile along the shore to the marina. Hikers get a sense of the past as they walk along an abandoned railroad bed to Wind Surf Beach. Two old freight cars and a water tower sit at the end of the trail.

Wind Surf Beach is about a mile north of the visitor center. Swimming is not permitted. Primitive camping is allowed along the west shore. The only facilities available are portable toilets. Future plans for this area include building a swim beach with picnic facilities.

Anglers enjoy excellent fishing at Navajo. The lake is known for

175

Directions:
Take U.S. Highway 160 west out of Pagosa Springs 17 miles. Turn south on Colorado Highway 151, go 18 miles to the town of Arboles, and turn south on Archuleta County Road 982 for 2 miles to the park entrance.

Phone or write:
Navajo State Park
Box 1697
Arboles, Colorado 81121
(303) 883-2208
San Juan Marina: (303) 731-4630
Ski school: (303) 371-4754

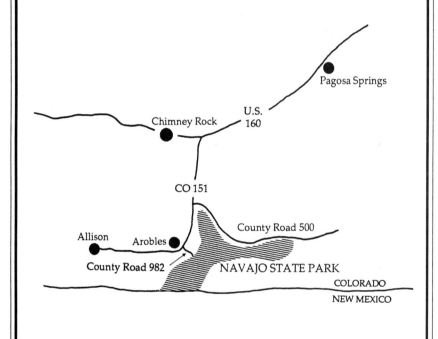

bluegill, catfish, crappie, and largemouth bass in the shallows along the water's edge. In the deeper, cooler waters, kokanee salmon and several varieties of trout are abundant. Visitors planning to fish in both Colorado and New Mexico must have fishing licenses for both states. Visitors will find six day-use areas along Archuleta County 500 on the north shoreline. Each site gives access to good fishing spots. The only facilities available are chemical toilets.

The rolling hills and flattop mesas surrounding Navajo are home to a variety of wild animals. Several species of waterfowl and shorebirds are found along the Piedra and San Juan rivers. Deer, elk, rabbits, and fox are common to the region. With a little luck, the careful observer may see coyotes and an occasional bobcat.

Paonia State Park

Situated in a steep narrow canyon at the eastern end of the North Fork Valley, Paonia State Park (formerly Paonia State Recreation Area) is surrounded by majestic mountains. The Raggeds Wilderness Area lies to the east, the West Elk Mountains lie to the south, Grand Mesa to the west, and White River National Forest to the north. At an elevation of 6,500 feet, the park is located only sixteen miles east of Paonia, Colorado. Its centerpiece, the Paonia Dam and Reservoir, was the first project of the Colorado River Storage Project, a basinwide system for development and use of water resources on the Upper Colorado River and its tributaries.

This is the most complex and extensive riverine water resource development in the world. It takes in the entire drainage of the Upper Colorado River Basin, encompassing parts of Colorado, Wyoming, Utah, Arizona, and New Mexico. Lake Powell, Flaming Gorge Reservoir, Navajo Lake, and Blue Mesa Reservoir are the largest reservoirs of the project. The main purpose of the reservoirs is to control the erratic water flow from the spring runoff and to ensure that water commitments to the Lower Basin states — California, Nevada, and Arizona — are met. The water is also used for agricultural, municipal, and industrial use in the Upper Basin.

Built by the U.S. Bureau of Reclamation, the Paonia Dam was dedicated in September 1962. Its main purposes are flood control, the collection and retention of silt washed in by Muddy Creek, and the irrigation of the North Fork Valley. The water quality of the lake is poor because a large amount of silt washes into the reservoir via Muddy Creek. Therefore, the lake does not support a diverse fish population. A few northern pike and trout can be caught from late June through August. The best luck is had by fly-fishermen around the confluence of Muddy Creek and Anthracite Creek below the dam.

Paonia State Park. Boating, water skiing, and sailing are the big attractions at Paonia between mid-June and mid-August, when the water level is high.

The recreational facilities were planned and built by the National Park Service between 1963 and 1966. The Colorado Division of Parks and Outdoor Recreation now manages these 1,507 acres of land and 337 acres of water, which became a state park in 1967. Because of the steep canyon walls, the recreation areas are restricted to the northern section of the park. Boating, waterskiing, jet skiing, and sailing are the big attractions between mid-June and mid-August, when the water level is high. The lake has one boat ramp located along the northeast shore with several picnic tables scattered around.

Paonia has two campgrounds that offer fifteen rustic campsites for tents, pickup campers, and small motor homes. The Spruce Campground has eight sites nestled below towering blue spruce trees between Colorado Highway 133 and Muddy Creek. The Hawsapple Campground lies on the east side of Muddy Creek along the north shoreline. Both campgrounds provide tables and grills at each site, with a vault toilet nearby. Drinking water is not available at Paonia, so campers are advised to bring their own.

The recreational facilities may be limited at Paonia, but the park is an excellent area for nature study. Paonia lies within the transition zone

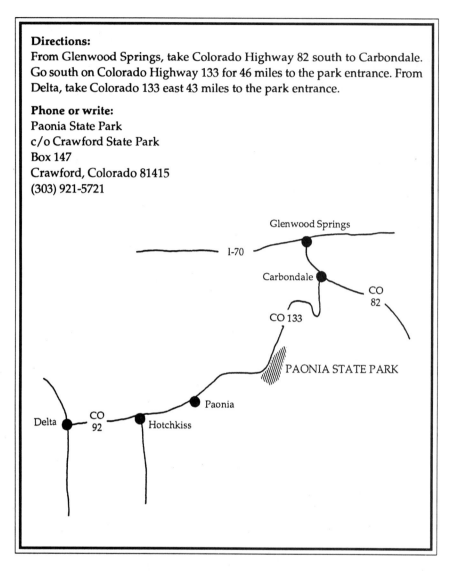

Directions:
From Glenwood Springs, take Colorado Highway 82 south to Carbondale.
Go south on Colorado Highway 133 for 46 miles to the park entrance. From
Delta, take Colorado 133 east 43 miles to the park entrance.

Phone or write:
Paonia State Park
c/o Crawford State Park
Box 147
Crawford, Colorado 81415
(303) 921-5721

between the Mesa Verde and Fort Union formations, which represent
two distinct geological eras. The section of the Mesa Verde Formation
found here was formed approximately 60 million to 130 million years
ago in the late Cretaceous Period, when western Colorado was part of a
large inland sea. The formation extends from the bottom of the dam
along the east side of the reservoir to Deep Creek.

The Fort Union Formation begins at Deep Creek along the east shore and extends northward beyond the park. The rocks from approximately 100 feet above the water level to the crest of the ridge belong to the Fort Union Formation, while the lower layers are from the Wasatch Formation. The latter were formed 50 million to 60 million years ago during the Paleocene Epoch, when the inland seas became landlocked and eventually turned into large fresh-water lakes.

Because this area lies in a transition zone, the surrounding hills are covered with dense vegetation. Narrowleaf cottonwoods, willows, and hawthorne trees with stands of Colorado blue spruce are the dominant trees along the riparian zone. Chokecherry thickets, clusters of mountain mahogany, gambel oak, and sagebrush follow the spruce and ponderosa pine up the rugged hillside. The slopes also blossom with an abundance of grasses and wildflowers during the summer months.

This variety of flora provides food and shelter for numerous animals. The careful observer can locate and photograph mule deer, squirrels, rabbits, coyotes, raccoons and marmots. With a little luck, one might see an occasional black bear during the late summer season feeding on the ripe wild berries.

Pearl Lake State Park

Imagine a quiet place in a pristine mountain setting, a place where the only sound is a gentle wind whispering through the pines, a place where the silence is so intense that you can almost hear your heart beat. Believe it or not, such a natural place does exist at Pearl Lake State Park, truly one of Colorado's best-kept secrets. Located in northern Routt County along the west side of the Continental Divide's Park Range, the 167-acre lake is ringed by rolling hills covered with stands of aspen trees and lodgepole pine.

Prior to the arrival of white explorers, northern Colorado was a summer and fall hunting ground for the Ute Indians. With the discovery of gold on nearby Hahns Peak and the arrival of miners in 1865, the Native Americans were slowly forced out of the region. Out of revenge they set fire to the surrounding mountains. Over a hundred years later, the charred forest has been rejuvenated with mature trees.

This was a productive mining region for several decades. As the industry faded out during the 1920s, sheepherders, cattle ranchers, and loggers moved into the region. Ever since, these three industries have provided the economic base for Northern Colorado — along with recreation.

Pearl Lake Dam was constructed over Lester Creek by the then–Game, Fish and Parks Department. The lake was built to provide recreation, mountain camping, and fishing in an aesthetic environment. It was called Lester Creek Reservoir State Recreation Area until 1972, when the name was changed in honor of Pearl Hartt, a local resident who was instrumental in the acquisition of land for the park. Mrs. Hartt's home was situated just west of the present park boundary. In 1988 Angelo Iacovetto, a retired businessman from Steamboat Springs, acquired the old Hartt home and relocated it closer to the water, where it stands

Pearl Lake State Park. The scenic beauty of Pearl Lake provides an ideal setting for canoeing.

today, remodeled and overlooking Pearl Lake. The refurbished Hartt home is on private property.

Recreational facilities at Pearl Lake are located along the northwest shore. The two camping loops provide thirty-nine sites nestled in a mature lodgepole pine forest. The campground can accommodate tents, pickup campers, and trailers. There are several pull-through sites; unfortunately, they are not big enough to handle large motor homes. Each campsite has a table and grill. Both flush and vault toilets are available.

South of the campground are the boat ramp and courtesy dock. Because of the relatively small size of the lake, only wakeless boating is allowed. The scenic beauty of Pearl Lake provides an ideal setting for canoeing. The placid atmosphere also makes Pearl a perfect setting for picnics. There are several tables near the campground and a couple more near the boat ramp.

Hiking opportunities are limited to the fishing paths that follow the shoreline. Visitors always enjoy the colorful display of wildflowers that carpet the lakeshore. Hikers who cross the dam on the south side of the lake are rewarded with a beautiful view of the lake and Farwell Mountain. Getting around the north end can be difficult. The meadow

Directions:
From Steamboat Springs, go west 2 miles on U.S. Highway 40 to Routt County Road 129, then turn right and go 23 miles to Pearl Lake Road. Turn east and go 2 miles to the park entrance.

Phone or write:
Pearl Lake State Park
c/o Steamboat Lake State Park
Box 750
Clark, Colorado 80428
(303) 879-3922

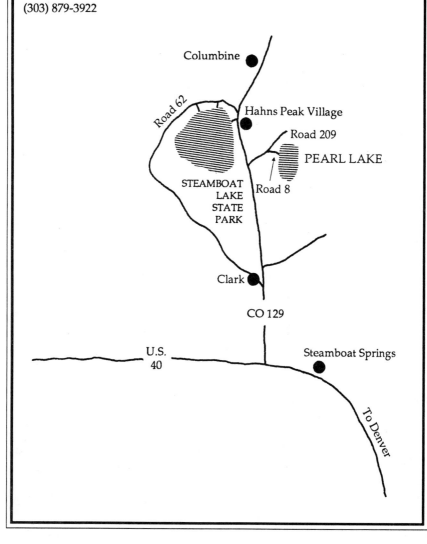

through which Lester Creek flows is usually wet and choked with thick clumps of willows.

Pearl's crystal-clear water has helped it become one of the best fisheries in the state. Anglers are delighted with the plentiful, large cutthroat trout that have been stocked by the Colorado Division of Wildlife. Fishermen may use only artificial flies and lures and must return any trout under fourteen inches. The limit on fish fourteen inches or over is two per person. In winter ice fishing can give anglers a memorable experience. However, the heavy snow on Pearl Lake Road is not plowed all the way to the lake. Cross-country skiing, snowshoeing, and snowmobiling are also fun winter activities at Pearl Lake.

The diversity of vegetation in northern Routt County provides good food and shelter for a variety of wildlife. By driving along Pearl Lake Road, visitors have an excellent chance to observe and photograph some of the 200 bird species populating the thick willows that thrive in the open meadows. Elk, mule deer, coyotes, beaver, and numerous other animals can be seen in this lush green valley.

Picnic Rock River Access Area

Early pioneers traveling west were faced with a big problem: the Rocky Mountains. Fur trappers and prospectors explored the many canyons along the Front Range and offered little encouragement to travelers heading west. It was not possible to pull wagons up the steep, narrow canyon walls. The easiest way to reach the West Coast was to travel around the mountains by one of two routes: the Oregon Trail to the north which passed through the open South Pass in Wyoming, or the Santa Fe Trail far south in New Mexico, where the mountains were not as high and rugged.

One route considered a possible shortcut to the west was along the Cache la Poudre River through the Poudre Canyon. In an effort to reach Brown's Park along the Green River, American Fur Company founder William Ashley pushed a trail up the steep canyon walls in 1824. In 1840 the trail was rerouted by a supply train destined for Fort Davy Crockett; this new trail was the basic route for today's U.S. Highway 287. In 1843 John Charles Fremont and guide Kit Carson, journeyed up the Poudre Canyon seeking easy passage over the Continental Divide. They found a new, easier trail later named Cameron Pass. This remains the primary route from Poudre Canyon over the Divide.

There are several colorful stories on how the river received the unusual French name "Cache la Poudre." The most popular story comes from Antoinne Janis, the first white settler in Larimer County. According to the story, in November 1836, Janis (then only twelve years old) was part of an American Fur Company supply train headed for the Green River from St. Louis. They were caught in a heavy snowstorm that lasted for several days, paralyzing the train. After the storm cleared, the party continued at a slow pace as the heavily loaded wagons bogged down in the snow. Orders were given to lighten the load, so the crew buried

186

THE CACHE LA POUDRE RIVER
DERIVES ITS NAME FROM
POWDER CACHED BY TRAPPERS
NEAR THIS SPOT – 1836
ERECTED BY CACHE LA POUDRE
CHAPTER, DAUGHTERS OF THE
AMERICAN REVOLUTION – 1910

Picnic Rock River Access Area. In 1910 the Daughters of the American Revolution erected a monument on the supposed site of the cache that inspired the name Cache la Poudre. The marker is located about three-fourths of a mile southeast of Bellvue along Bingham Hill Road.

expendable goods, including gunpowder. The train continued its journey to the Green River; later, several men returned to recover the cached supplies and gunpowder. Thus, the story claims, the river became the "cache of the powder," or Cache la Poudre.

Making the story more interesting is the fact that the name Cache la Poudre was used in a journal written by Captain John Grant of the federal government's Dodge Expedition in 1835, a year before the alleged burying of the powder in Janis's story. Despite this inconsistency, the Daughters of the American Revolution erected a monument on the supposed site of the Cache in 1910. The marker is located about three-quaters of a mile southeast of Bellvue along Bingham Hill Road.

However the river got its name, the Cache la Poudre's water is in great demand. It is used not only for urban development on the plains but also for recreation in the canyon. In 1986 the river became the only one on the Front Range protected under the National Wild and Scenic Rivers Act. Under this designation, seventy-five miles of the Cache la Poudre and its tributaries have been preserved for future generations. The river offers a wide variety of recreational activities. One popular area lies along Colorado Highway 14: Picnic Rock River Access Area. This site, twelve miles northwest of Fort Collins, is used by anglers, rafters, kayakers, and picnickers.

Two entities share ownership of the land at Picnic Rock. The city of Fort Collins owns roughly three acres, while the rest is owned by the Colorado Division of Wildlife. In the spring of 1987, the Colorado Division of Parks and Outdoor Recreation assumed management of the site through a memorandum of understanding with the Division of Wildlife and a lease agreement with the city of Fort Collins.

There are two sections to the Picnic Rock River Access Area, the Upper and Lower Picnic Rock sites. A distance of approximately a quarter-mile separates the two. Besides being a popular take-out area for river rafters and kayakers, both Upper and Lower sites are popular picnic areas. Tables, grills, and vault toilets are available for public use. Upper Picnic Rock provides covered picnic cabanas.

West of the Picnic Rock River Access Area, the Poudre Canyon offers a variety of outdoor activities. Numerous hiking trails lead through colorful backcountry. Trailheads to the Grey Rock, Hewlet Gulch, Mt. McConnel, Dadd Gulch, and other trails can be found along Colorado 14. The river itself offers exciting whitewater boating, with rapids ranging from Class II to Class VI. Boaters are advised to know the

Directions:
From Fort Collins, go north on U.S. Highway 287 to Colorado Highway 14, then west for 3 miles to the entrance.

Phone or write:
Picnic Rock River Access Area
c/o Lory State Park
708 Lodgepole Drive
Bellvue, Colorado 80512
(303) 493-1623

stretches of river they plan to run. Each canoe, kayak, or raft must display the owner's name and address.

The river corridor provides excellent habitat for a variety of animal species. The early morning and evening hours are the best times for viewing bighorn sheep, mule deer, elk, black bear, and an occasional mountain lion.

Fishing along the Cache la Poudre is some of the best in Colorado. Brown, rainbow, and brook trout are abundant, as the Division of Wildlife stocks over 53,000 trout annually.

Ridgway State Park

Ridgway State Park (formerly Ridgway State Recreation Area), twenty miles south of Montrose in the Uncompahgre Valley, is surrounded by 14,000-foot mountains. Its picturesque scenery is some of the best in Colorado, with Mount Sneffels and the San Juan Mountains to the south, the Cimarron Mountains to the east, and the Uncompahgre Plateau to the northwest. In addition to natural beauty, Ridgway has ultra-modern accommodations built with the future in mind. Ridgway's facilities for handicapped visitors are the best in the state, perhaps the country. Eighty percent of the campsites, most of the picnic areas, the swim beach, and other recreation sites are accessible to those who are physically disabled. Ridgway Dam and Reservoir are the result of the Dallas Creek Project, which was first proposed in 1951. Land acquisition delays and a long debate over where and how to build the dam held up the start of construction until 1978. The dam was dedicated on August 22, 1987. Built by the U.S. Bureau of Reclamation in cooperation with the Tri-County Water Conservancy District, Ridgway is now the principal unit of the Dallas Creek Project. Its primary purpose is to provide water for municipal and industrial use, irrigation, and recreation. The lake, nearly five miles long and roughly a mile wide, is fed by the Uncompahgre River, Dallas Creek, and Alkali Creek. When full, the reservoir holds 80,000 acre-feet of water.

The early history of the Uncompahgre Valley goes back to the late 1800s, when rumors of gold strikes and untold riches lying buried in the majestic San Juan Mountains brought scores of speculators to the area. By the late 1870s, several camps and towns had sprung up in a once-serene area. The small, but thriving community of Dallas was located near the confluence of the Uncompahgre River and Dallas Creek. A census taken in 1880 showed that most of the adult males living in the area were farmers and ranchers. Relatively few of the residents were associated with the mining industry. In 1887 the Denver and Rio Grande Railroad made Dallas the transportation hub of the northwestern side of the San Juan Mountains, and the town became the shipping point to Telluride and other areas in southwestern Colorado. The famous freighter David Wood operated his business from this booming community.

Most of Dallas was destroyed by a disastrous fire in 1888; in 1891 the railroad decided to make Ridgway its new transportation hub, bringing an end to the once-proud community. Part of the site of the former town has now been inundated by the Ridgway Reservoir.

With the demise of Dallas during the early 1890s, the small town of Ridgway began to prosper. The Rio Grande Southern set out to extend the railroad 175 miles to Durango in an effort to expand service to the mining industry. The company was only three years old when the Silver Panic of 1893 forced it into receivership. The bankrupt railroad was purchased by the Denver and Rio Grande, which used the tracks to serve the cattle industry.

The combination of mining, agriculture, and the railroad made Ridgway a typical Western town. In 1891 there were five saloons, a weekly newspaper, a bank, a creamery, a church, and several hotels and businesses. Despite the rapid growth, the town failed to plan for the future. Children attended school in a blacksmith shop until better facilities were arranged in a hotel. Finally, in 1899, a new schoolhouse was completed.

One of the strangest locomotives ever seen, the "Galloping Goose," was built in Ridgway in 1931 as a means of transporting freight, mail, and passengers. It was built from a Buick Master Six touring car; its trunk, tires, bumpers, and axles were removed and replaced by flanged railroad wheels, cowcatchers, special lights, and a horn that sounded like a honking goose. The Goose could travel from Ridgway to Durango in nine hours, allowing the railroad to operate economically until 1950, when the mail contract was lost. In 1952 the railroad was dismantled and sold for scrap.

As useful as the Goose was, only seven of these machines were built. Six of them are still intact and can be viewed by the public. Engine Number 1 was dismantled; Engines Number 2, 6, and 7 are at the Colorado Railroad Museum in Golden; Engine Number 3 is in Knotts Berry

Ridgway State Park. There were only seven Galloping Goose engines built. Engine Number 7 is on display at the Colorado Railroad Museum in Golden.

Farm in California; Engine Number 4 is on display at Telluride; and Engine Number 5 is preserved at Delores, Colorado, by the Galloping Goose Historical Society.

Ridgway was opened as a state park on August 28, 1989. The recreational facilities of this 3,260-acre park were designed and built by the Colorado Division of Parks and Outdoor Recreation and funded by the Bureau of Reclamation. For better service to the public, the park has been divided into four separate recreation sites: Dutch Charlie, Dallas Creek, San Juan Overlook, and Cow Creek.

The best way to get acquainted with Ridgway is to tour the visitor center at the Dutch Charlie area near the park entrance. The visitor center has several display panels illustrating the history, wildlife, and geology of the park and surrounding area. Park rangers will answer questions and provide information to travelers passing through southwest Colorado. From the south side of the visitor center, a cement walkway extends about 200 yards to a redwood deck. From here the view is magnificent: Deep blue water covers the valley floor, and the snowcapped peaks of the San Juan Mountains rise in the background.

Ridgway State Park. The best way to get acquainted with Ridgway is to visit the visitor center at the Dutch Charlie area near the entrance station. The center has several display panels that illustrate the history, wildlife, and geology of the park and surrounding area.

Dutch Charlie has two ultramodern campgrounds — the Elk Ridge Campground high upon a piñon-covered hill overlooking the lake, and the Dakota Terrace Campground on the hillside between the park entrance and the marina. The two campgrounds provide 187 campsites, including 10 walk-in tent sites, each with a level, sanded tent pad. Several campsites have elevated wooden decks designed for handicapped campers. All sites are equipped with a table, grill, and an electrical hookup. Additional facilities include flush toilets, showers, a laundry, water hydrants, and soft drink machines. A dump station is located near the Dakota Terrace entrance.

Ridgway's boat ramp and marina can be reached via Marina Road at the northeast corner of the Dutch Charlie area. The marina offers boat and slip rental, fuel, a fish-cleaning station, and boating and fishing accessories. Ridgway is rapidly becoming famous for its trout fishing. The Division of Wildlife periodically stocks the lake with rainbow trout. Anglers are challenged by the abundance of brown trout that originally inhabited the Uncompahgre River prior to the construction of the dam.

The large swim beach and greenbelt area delight sun worshipers looking to soak up the warm Colorado sun. There is no lifeguard on

Ridgway State Park. The modern facilities at Ridgway include elevated wooden decks at several of the campsites.

duty, and children under twelve must be accompanied by an adult. The beach house has changing rooms with lockers and showers. A gently sloping walk designed for wheelchairs meanders down through the swimming area, separating the beach and the grassy lawn, before reaching a children's playground.

Just south of the swim beach, visitors will find a fishing access trail that follows the shoreline around a knoll. Numerous picnic tables with grills line the trail. Several more sheltered tables can be found along Shoreline Road, which begins at the marina parking area.

Dutch Charlie has roughly three miles of trails that connect with each of the other recreational areas. From the deck below the visitor center, the cement walkway becomes a gravel trail that leads to the Elk Ridge Campground, then down a steep hill to the marina and swim beach. The trail then passes through to the Dakota Terrace Campground before returning to the visitor center.

The Dallas Creek day-use area, which is still under construction, is located at the south end of the park near the confluence of the Uncompahgre River and Dallas Creek. Scattered across the reservoir's east shore are numerous picnic tables and a group picnic area. There is no

Ridgway State Park. Visitors are delighted with the large swim beach and greenbelt, where sun worshipers can soak up the warm Colorado rays. The beach house has a changing room with lockers and showers.

designated boat ramp at Dallas Creek; however, there is a boat launching site for canoes, sailboards, and other hand-carried vessels. A pedestrian bridge extends across the river and provides fishing access to the west bank.

Perched high upon a hill east of U.S. Highway 550 is the future site of the San Juan Overlook. Upon completion, it will have numerous picnic sites where visitors can enjoy a 360-degree panoramic view of the park and surrounding mountains.

The Pa Co Chu Puk (an Indian word for "cow creek") area is located west of U.S. Highway 550 below the dam, situated in the riparian zone along the Uncompahgre River and Cow Creek. This area is under construction. It will eventually offer eighty-five new campsites with full hookups and fifteen walk-in tent sites. A nominal fee will be charged for electrical, water, and sewer hookups. Day-use facilities are to include several individual picnic sites and a group picnic area. A number of new trails will be built, along with a footbridge to provide access to both sides of the river.

Directions:
From Montrose, drive 20 miles south on U.S. Highway 550 to the park entrance.

Phone or write:
Ridgway State Park
28555 Highway 550
Ridgway, Colorado 81432
(303) 626-5822

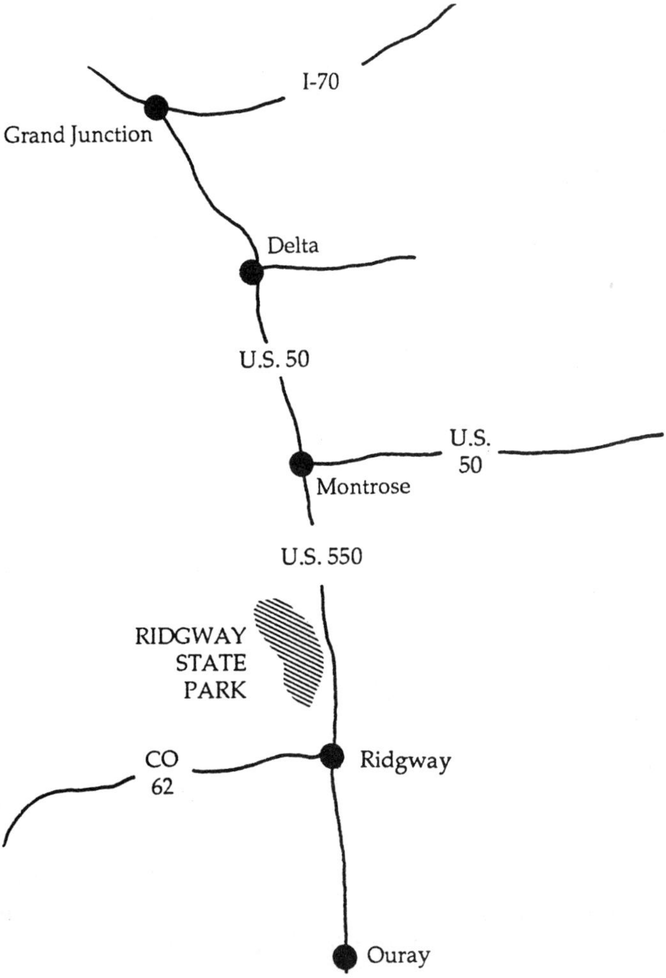

I-70

Grand Junction

Delta

U.S. 50

U.S. 50

Montrose

U.S. 550

RIDGWAY
STATE
PARK

CO
62

Ridgway

Ouray

These new recreation areas are being built with conveniences for handicapped visitors. When construction is completed, Ridgway will become one of the largest and most modern parks on the Western Slope. It will offer virtually unlimited opportunities for fishing, water sports, camping, picnicking, biking, and nature study. Ridgway will provide an interconnecting trail system for hiking, jogging, and biking that will meander through the park and link all four recreation areas.

The names chosen for the four recreation areas at Ridgway were voted on by local school children. The Dutch Charlie area was named, logically enough, after an old Dutchman named Charlie. During the late 1800s, Charlie operated a blacksmith shop, boardinghouse, and livery stable along Alkali Creek near the present-day marina and boat ramp. To avoid public confusion, the Pa Co Chu Puk area will be referred to as Cow Creek.

Rifle Falls State Park

For people who have not had the opportunity to see the waterfalls and lush green mountains of Hawaii, Rifle Falls State Park is the next best place. The triple waterfall created by East Rifle Creek as it flows over a limestone cliff with its mysterious caves has affectionately been named "Colorado's Hawaii." Water thunders over the cliff as a misty spray drenches the grass and moss-covered rocks below, creating a placid, almost tropical paradise in an arid region.

Geologists believe the cliff was originally a large beaver dam. The stagnant water retained by the dam was saturated with chemicals, mainly calcium salts, which eventually transformed the beaver dam into a large limestone cliff. The falls themselves are unnatural. Originally, East Rifle Creek sent a wall of water over the entire cliff, which forms a gradual S shape about 100 yards long. In 1910 the town of Rifle built the Rifle Hydroelectric Plant over East Rifle Creek, altering the natural flow to its present course. The Rifle plant was the first hydroelectric power station in Colorado. Public Service Company bought the plant in 1915 and operated it until 1952. All of the generating equipment was removed at that time; the old stone buildings above the falls were dismantled in 1971.

Nearly a century earlier, the area was first settled by James "Cup" Watson, who filed a claim on 160 acres of land that contained Rifle Falls. Watson built several cabins on the property and rented them to tourists, calling his place the Rifle Falls Ranch. While exploring his land, he found the caves under the falls. Although the caves were small, the interior walls were lined with beautiful but delicate stalactites and stalagmites. Watson built a door around the entrance to each cave and charged visitors twenty-five cents to view them. To attract more business, Watson provided transportation to and from the ranch in a one-horse buggy.

198

Rifle Falls State Park. The Coyote Trail leads visitors along the base of the cliffs to the limestone caves.

Directions:
Take Interstate 70 to the Rifle exit. Follow Colorado Highway 13 north and drive 3 miles beyond Rifle; then turn east on Colorado Highway 325 and drive 5 miles to Rifle Gap State Park. Continue on Colorado 325 past Rifle Gap for 4.8 miles to the park entrance.

Phone or write:
Rifle Falls State Park
c/o Rifle Gap State Park
0050 County Road 219
Rifle, Colorado 81650
(303) 625-1607

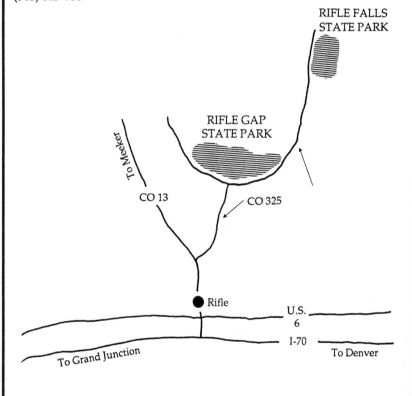

The land north of Rifle Falls was owned by Walter Wilder, while Allen Zerbe settled south of the Rifle Falls Ranch. During the early 1890s, Zerbe purchased the Rifle Falls Ranch from Watson, leased the Wilder property, and converted the whole valley into a swank tourist resort. The resort was destroyed by fire around the turn of the century and was never rebuilt.

Today, Rifle Falls is a forty-acre park managed by the Colorado Division of Parks and Outdoor Recreation. This cool, peaceful place is truly a gem in the state park system. It offers excellent opportunites for hiking, picnicking, and camping.

Rifle Falls has two camping areas. There are eleven drive-in campsites that can accommodate trailers, pickup campers, and motor homes north of the park entrance; south of it are seven walk-in sites for tents. All campsites are equipped with a table and grill. Additional facilities include vault toilets and water hydrants. Neither a dump station nor electrical hookups are available. The north campground is adjacent to a small day-use area where visitors will find several picnic tables shaded by tall cottonwood trees.

Rifle Falls has two trails that can be hiked in about thirty-five minutes each. The Coyote Trail begins near the falls and follows the base of the cliff to the caves. Then it climbs up a steep hill to the top of the cliff and continues along the rim to the falls. From here the skeletal remains of the old power plant are visible. Looking down over the falls, visitors have a scenic view of the lush valley below. The trail becomes steep as it leads back down into the valley, and if the soil is wet, footing can become very uncertain.

The Squirrel Trail begins next to the day-use area. It meanders southward along the riparian zone beneath the tall box elders and narrowleaf cottonwoods, crosses East Rifle Creek, and turns north, continuing through the walk-in camping area before returning to the entrance station.

Rifle Gap State Park

Driving north of Rifle along Colorado Highway 325, a road that was once part of the Ute Trail, motorists come upon one of Colorado's most unique geographic features: the Grand Hogback. This ridge extends north to Meeker and slowly turns southeast toward New Castle; many people consider it the geographic boundary between the Rocky Mountains and the Colorado Plateau. The Grand Hogback received its name from members of the Hayden Survey Party and A. C. Peale, a geologist for the party, as they explored the region in 1876. Rifle Creek and Colorado 325 cut through a natural notch of near-vertical rock formations. This notch, called Rifle Gap, is the gateway to Rifle Gap State Park (formerly Rifle Gap State Recreation Area).

Old-timers tell stories of the early cattle drives through the area. Herds would assemble at a roundup ground at the south end of Ward Gulch where three streams join to form Rifle Creek. The stream flows south toward the town of Rifle through the Grand Hogback, where the cowboys would fire guns into the air to signal their approach to distant herds.

At the confluence of West Rifle Creek and East Rifle Creek sat a town named Austin. Stagecoaches traveling along the Ute Trail would stop in Austin to change horses and allow passengers to eat and freshen up. By the turn of the century, many Austin residents had relocated to nearby Rifle to be closer to the Grand River (now the Colorado River) and the railroad. Only a few mine dumps and cabins remained of the town when construction of the Rifle Gap Dam began in 1964. The only building left was the schoolhouse, which operated from 1887 to 1958. (The original school was actually a small log cabin that was destroyed by fire. A new wood-frame school and library were built in 1916.) During construction of the dam, the school was moved south of Rifle Gap and

Rifle Gap State Park. The town of Austin was inundated by the Rifle Gap Reservoir during the 1960s. The only building to survive was the schoolhouse, which was moved to the Silt Historical Park in 1987.

used as a museum. In 1987 the old school was moved to Silt, where it is now on display at the Silt Historical Park.

The Rifle Gap Dam and Reservoir were built by the U.S. Bureau of Reclamation in conjunction with the Silt Water Conservancy District and were completed in 1968. The main purpose of the reservoir was to provide water for the farmers and ranchers in the Rifle area. Water was first drawn from the reservoir for irrigation in 1969.

Rifle Gap became a state park in September 1967. At that time the Colorado Game, Fish and Parks Department obtained a memorandum of agreement and the right to manage the recreation facilities. The park is now managed by the Colorado Division of Parks and Outdoor Recreation. At 6,000 feet above sea level, the reservoir is surrounded by mountains covered with Utah cedar and piñon pine. The lower valleys burst forth with an abundance of sagebrush, greasewood, tamarisk, and rabbitbrush. With fishing, water sports, and camping as the major attractions, the 1,305-acre park is truly a place for all outdoor enthusiasts.

In May 1971 Rifle Gap became a place for art enthusiasts, too. An artist named Christo Javacheff began construction on a project that

Rifle Gap State Park. In May 1971 Rifle Gap received considerable attention when artist Christo Javacheff attempted to build a curtain across the natural gap in the Grand Hogback.

became known as Christo's Curtain. On the north side of the gap, he extended huge cables from one side of the canyon to the other. From these cables he intended to suspend a copper-orange curtain made of nylon polyamide across the gap. A large semicircular opening would allow cars to pass beneath the curtain on Colorado 325. But after five months of hard work, the project failed. Strong, gusty winds shredded the curtain into pieces just one day before it was to be hung on the cables.

Javacheff would not admit defeat. He decided to try again a year later, and on August 10, 1972, the giant curtain was unfurled. However, Javacheff's victory did not last long. Twenty-eight hours later, gusty winds again ripped the curtain apart. Although badly damaged, the curtain drew curious visitors until it was removed two weeks later.

Fishermen generally have better luck at Rifle Gap than artists. Anglers enjoy the abundance of rainbow and German brown trout, walleye, and large and smallmouth bass that are periodically stocked by the Colorado Division of Wildlife. For cold-weather buffs, Rifle Gap offers some of the best ice fishing in the state during the winter months.

Directions:
Take Interstate 70 and exit onto Colorado Highway 13. Drive north 3 miles beyond Rifle, turn right on Colorado Highway 325, and drive 5 miles to the park entrance.

Phone or write:
Rifle Gap State Park
0050 County Road 219
Rifle, Colorado 81650
(303) 625-1607

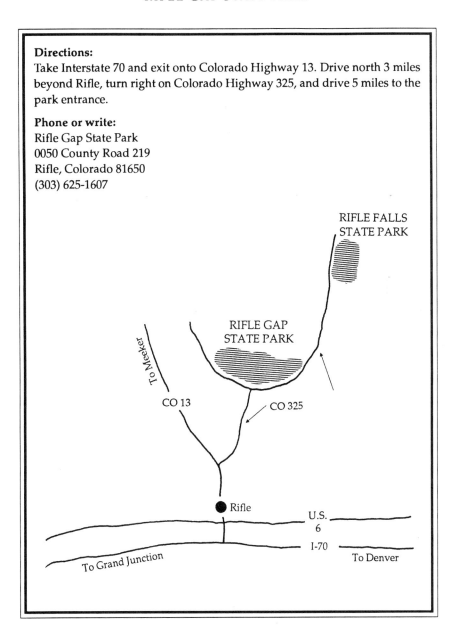

Visitors will find several fishing areas on the south side of the lake. At the southeast area along Garfield County Road 252 is the Brown parking area. The Chinook parking area at the intersection of Garfield County 252 and Colorado 325, overlooks the reservoir. From here there is a majestic view of the lake and the mountains to the north and a clear view of the famous Rifle Gap to the south. Two more parking areas, Perch and Walleye, are located east of the dam along Colorado 325. About halfway between the Walleye parking lot and the main park entrance, a dirt road leads to the Bass day-use area along the east shore.

Most of the recreational facilities are centered around the large boat ramp on the north shore. Visitors will find a swim beach along the northwest shore; no lifeguard is on duty, so individuals swim at their own risk. Next to the swimming area is a water ski take-off/drop-off area. Jet skiing, sailing, windsurfing, and scuba diving are other popular water sports at Rifle Gap.

The park has four separate campgrounds with forty-six campsites suitable for tents, trailers, pickup campers, and motor homes. The Sage Campground lies just north of the boat ramp; the Piñon and Cedar campgrounds are found east of the boat ramp; and the Cottonwood Campground is located along the northeast corner of the lake. All four campgrounds provide tables and grills at each site, with water hydrants and vault toilets nearby. (The Sage Campground also has sheltered tables.) The dump station for all four campgrounds is next to the Cottonwood entrance. Electrical hookups are not available. During the autumn hunting season, the campgrounds are often used as a base by big-game hunters who pursue deer and elk in neighboring White River National Forest.

Day-use facilities along the north shore include six separate picnic areas. The Magpie and Heron picnic grounds are found to the northeast, near the Cottonwood Campground; the Mallard and Teal picnic areas are next to the loop road that passes through the Cedar Campground; and the Eagle and Hawk picnic areas are centrally located near the entrance to the boat ramp.

The state is trying to purchase land north of the present boundary. The additional property would allow the construction of new campgrounds with modern conveniences. Plans are being made to build hiking, bicycling, and cross-country skiing trails, tubing and sledding runs, and a safe and secure fishing jetty for those with physical handicaps.

Roxborough State Park

Because of its unique geology and diverse ecosystem, in 1979 Roxborough became the first state park to be designated a Colorado Natural Area. The following year it received National Natural Landmark designation from the U.S. Department of the Interior. Unlike its cousins — Red Rocks to the north and Garden of the Gods to the south — Roxborough has no graffiti marring its russet boulders and no roads disturbing the placid beauty. The purpose of the park is to protect the area's unique scenery and resources while providing opportunities for hiking and learning about Colorado's heritage. It's a park where visitors just look and listen to the sounds of nature.

As early as 1910, Denver Mayor Robert Speer felt that Roxborough should be owned by the city "for the free use of the people." The property was held by the Roxborough Land Company, and neither the state of Colorado nor the city of Denver could raise the mere $6,000 needed to purchase it. The land was situated around the old Henry S. Persse homestead (located in the northeast corner of the present park); after the death of John Persse (Henry's son), the land was bought by the Helmer family in 1921.

In 1967 the land was sold to the Woodmoor Corporation, a company that envisioned a housing development among the historic rocks. The company filed for bankruptcy in 1975, and the state of Colorado was able to purchase 500 acres. Additional land purchases brought the size of the park to its present 1,620 acres.

Located approximately twenty-five miles southwest of Denver, Roxborough became a state park in 1975. However, because of access problems, more than a decade passed before it finally opened to the public. The George T. O'Malley Visitor Center was dedicated in May of

Roxborough State Park. The George T. O'Malley Visitor Center was dedicated in May 1986.

1986. On May 15, 1987, Roxborough opened its gates, welcoming guests to explore seven identified ecosystems and just about every type of natural environment present along the Colorado Front Range. Roxborough has often been referred to as the "city of rocks." More than 1.2 billion years of geologic time are represented by the spectacular rock formations found within Roxborough. Carpenter Peak, the highest point in the park at 7,200 feet, is made of gneiss, banded crystalline rocks, and granite from the Precambrian Era, the oldest division of geologic time. The massive red rocks that Roxborough is known for come from the Fountain Formation. They were formed by stream-deposited sand and gravel eroded from the ancestral Rockies some 300 million years ago. On the east side of the park is the Dakota Hogback, a jagged ridge of sandstone laid down as flood plains and beaches during the Cretaceous Period some 135 million years ago. The Lyons Formation, which lies between the hogback and the Fountain Formation, was once a series of sand dunes located along the shores of ancient seas.

Originally these formations were all deposited horizontally, but they were tilted skyward during the birth of the Rocky Mountains some

Roxborough State Park. Roxborough has been referred to as the "city of rocks." More than 1.2 billion years of geologic time are encompassed by the spectacular rock formations found at Roxborough.

70 million years ago in the Tertiary Period. Over the years the rocks and ridges have been sculpted by water, wind, and weather.

Roxborough is in a transition zone where the plains meet the mountains. The area's geological structure has resulted in microclimates that have produced seven distinct plant communities in a unique mixture of prairie and mountain species. Gambel oak cling to the hillsides and along the giant rocks. Yucca and prickly pear cactus thrive on the dry grassland, where water is scarce. Tall, lush grasses and a variety of wildflowers, such as Indian paintbrush, golden banner, and penstemon, swing with the gentle breeze in the wet meadows. Cottonwoods and box elders grow along the banks of the intermittently flowing Little Willow Creek. A grove of aspens is found at the surprisingly low elevation of 6,200 feet; this cluster may be a holdover from the last ice age, when the climate in Colorado was cooler. Along the slopes of Carpenter Peak, ponderosa pine and Douglas fir survive below their normal elevations. Even the massive rocks give life, supporting a variety of lichens and moss.

The facilities at Roxborough are purposely limited to the visitor center and the trail system to minimize the human impact on the environment. Rock climbing and camping are prohibited, and family pets are not allowed in the park. Nor does the park provide a picnic area, although visitors are welcome to pack a lunch and eat at one of the benches at the visitor center or along the trails. Roxborough does have a "people mover," an oversized golf cart designed to carry the handicapped and elderly. Up to eight people can enjoy the natural beauty of the Fountain Valley Trail as they ride around on the vehicle.

Park rangers and naturalists provide guided nature tours for schoolchildren, youth clubs, and senior citizen groups. School groups are often booked six months ahead; weekend activities are available with a month's notice.

Roxborough has over twelve miles of hiking trails. The most popular route is the 2.3-mile Fountain Valley Trail. The trail runs north along Fountain Valley to the Persse's historic 1901 homestead, then turns south between the Dakota Hogback and the Lyons Formation toward the visitor center. The Lyons Trail, a spur from the Fountain Valley Trail, climbs up a hogback for half a mile and offers a splendid view of Fountain Valley. The mile-long Willow Creek Trail guides hikers through a cluster of gambel oak and across open meadows full of wildflowers. The park's

Directions:
From Denver, take U.S. Highway 85 (Santa Fe Drive) south to Titan Road. Turn right and go 3.5 miles. Then turn left (still on Titan Road) and go 1.3 miles to an intersection, where the road turns into Rampart Range Road. Continue south for 2.4 miles, turn left on Roxborough Park Road, and turn right into the park next to the fire station.

Phone or write:
Roxborough State Park
4751 N. Roxborough Drive
Littleton, Colorado 80125
(303) 973-3959

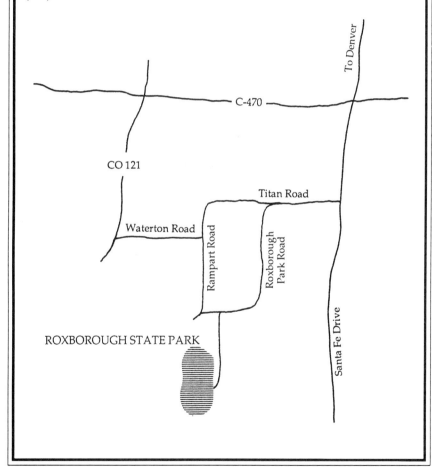

longest trail, the Carpenter Peak Trail, is a 5.5-mile hike over moderate to steep terrain. Once at the summit, hikers are rewarded with a spectacular view in all directions. From near the top of Carpenter Peak, a 4.5-mile trail extends down into Waterton Canyon and joins the famous Colorado Trail. Another path with good views, the South Rim Overlook Trail, is a 1.5-mile path from the visitor center into the southern half of the park. From the overlook, observers can easily identify the Fountain Formation, the Lyons Formation, and the Dakota Hogback.

Spinney Mountain State Park

Spinney Mountain State Park (formerly Spinney Mountain State Recreation Area) rests at 8,686 feet above sea level with the snowcapped Collegiate Peaks to the west, Thirty-nine-mile Mountain to the south, and the isolated Spinney Mountain to the north. Lying at the southern tip of South Park, Spinney Mountain State Park shares its early history with Eleven Mile State Park, its neighbor to the east. Archaeological evidence indicates that the Folsom, Plano, Archaic, and Woodland prehistoric cultures inhabited the area about 12,000 years ago. The lifestyle of these early cultures was continued by the Ute Indians who dominated the mountainous regions of Colorado as early as A.D. 1000. The only remaining historical sites in the area are linked to the intrusion of the white man, beginning with the French fur trappers, followed by the Spanish expeditions during the 1700s. After the Colorado gold rush began in 1859, the landscape of South Park changed dramatically. Mines and mining towns sprang up around the edges of the valley, and the Ute hunting grounds near the center of the valley were transformed into ranchland.

To provide better access into and through South Park, the Colorado Midland Railroad was extended into the region and operated between 1887 and 1918. The train was popular with tourists, who participated on one-day wildflower-viewing excursions into South Park. The train followed a route from Colorado Springs through Eleven Mile Canyon along the South Platte River where wildflowers were abundant, to the Spinney railroad station just east of today's Spinney Mountain Reservoir, where it turned around and returned to the city.

According to a 1891 census, the small community of Spinney had a population of twenty people. Unfortunately, there are no longer any

213

Spinney Mountain State Park. Spinney Mountain Reservoir has developed a reputation for rewarding anglers with trophy fish. The cold mountain water is home to rainbow, brown, and cutthroat trout, as well as northern pike.

visible remains of the small village; it disappeared shortly after the railroad was replaced by U.S. Highway 24 in the early part of the century.

Very little development took place in South Park during the ensuing decade. Ranching came to dominate the economy of the valley, which remained sparsely populated. Over time, recreation emerged as an important economic factor, as hunters and fishermen paid increasing numbers of visits to the area.

Construction of Spinney Mountain Dam over the South Platte River was completed in 1981 and dedicated in 1982 by the city of Aurora. The area was opened to the public the following year as a recreation area. The reservoir, with its 2,520 acres of water, was leased to the Division of Parks and Outdoor Recreation in March 1988 by the city of Aurora. The park is strictly a day-use area, opening half an hour before sunrise and closing one hour after sunset from May 1, when the ice has usually melted, through November 15, which is about when the lake freezes over.

The openness of the rolling and flat ground around Spinney Mountain resembles a shortgrass prairie, a unique but delicate ecosystem that

Directions:
From Colorado Springs, take U.S. Highway 24 west for 55 miles over Wilkerson Pass. Turn left on Park County Road 23, go 2.8 miles, turn right on Park County Road 59, and go 1.1 miles to the park entrance.

Phone or write:
Spinney Mountain State Park
c/o Eleven Mile State Park
Star Route 2, Box 4229
Lake George, Colorado 80827
(719) 748-3401

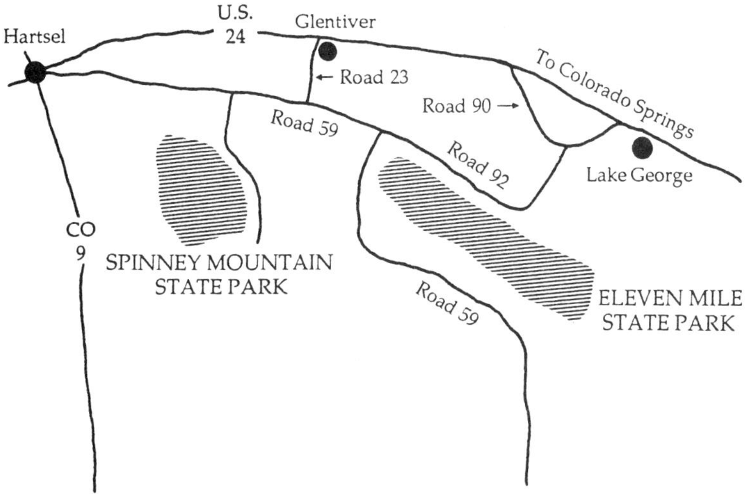

is sensitive to human activity. Wildflowers and plants overrun this area; a few of the more common species are rabbitbrush, sagebrush, sticky asters, scarlet gilia, and Indian paintbrush.

Along the northwest shore, a series of small islands that creates a natural habitat for nesting birds and waterfowl. The most common species are Canadian geese, ducks, and western grebes. This area is off limits to visitors during the nesting season. The hunting of waterfowl and small game is permitted at Spinney during the regular hunting season, usually from October until the park closes in mid-November.

Spinney Mountain Reservoir has developed a reputation for rewarding anglers with trophy fish. The cold mountain water abounds with rainbow, brown, and cutthroat trout, as well as northern pike. Anglers can keep only one trout, which must be at least twenty inches long. The limit on northern pike is twenty fish, but there are no size restrictions. Only artificial flies and lures are permitted.

Two boat ramps serve the reservoir, one on the northeast shore, the other along the southeast shore. Boaters are advised to use caution while on the lake. Strong, gusty winds reaching thirty to forty miles per hour are common, creating four- to five-foot waves. Because of the 8,000-foot elevation, the water is usually cold; therefore, water-contact sports such as swimming, waterskiing, wading, and scuba diving are prohibited. Windsurfing is permitted only when the participant is wearing a full wet suit or dry suit.

Picnicking is permitted anywhere in the park. Several picnic sites along the northern and southern shores provide tables and fire rings. The area directly north and east of the dam is closed to the public. It is reserved as a maintenance and residential area for the city of Aurora employees who maintain the dam.

Stagecoach State Park

Stagecoach State Park lies in an area the Ute Indians called *Egeria*, meaning "crooked woman," to describe the winding course of the Yampa River through the valley. Located approximately sixteen miles south of Steamboat Springs and four miles east of Oak Creek in Routt County, Stagecoach is rapidly becoming a favorite park for many Colorado residents.

Settlement of the Upper Yampa Valley did not begin until the late nineteenth century. The early settlers were attracted to northwest Colorado for its agricultural potential. However, coal mining had become the major industry by the turn of the century. Abandoned and active coal mining operations dot the landscape around the town of Oak Creek. There are still four mines operating in Routt County, including the Edna Mine, the oldest active one in Colorado.

Stagecoach Dam and Reservoir were built by the Upper Yampa Water Conservancy District. The Colorado legislature passed House Bill 1102 in 1983, allowing the Colorado Water Conservation Board to make a low-interest loan to fund the project. Completed in 1989, the project is used for water storage and irrigation. The dam is uniquely constructed over the Yampa River, using roller-compacted concrete with erosion-resistant rock abutments. At the base of the dam is an 800-kilowatt generating power plant.

The name "stagecoach" originated from developer Steve Arnold of the Woodmoor Corporation, who initiated the property development south of the reservoir. A year-round resort with condominiums, a ski hill, and a lake was planned in the 1970s. Financial problems have kept the project from reaching completion. Several condominiums were built along the south shore; approximately 1,500 people will live there when the development is finally done. Several historical landmarks have been

217

identified in the Stagecoach area, although none of them qualifies as a registered state historical site. A mail and stage route ran down Little Morrison Creek through the canyon below the dam. Today's Routt County Road 14, which goes over Yellow Jacket Pass, was once part of the stage route. Yellow Jacket Pass was supposedly named for the many wasps found in the area; another story claims that an outlaw wearing a yellow jacket used the vicinity as a hideout. The Yellow Jacket schoolhouse once located near the southern park entrance, was used until 1958, while the Yellow Jacket Grange Hall, which served as a local community center, stood near the park's main entrance, as did a stage stop and rest area built across from the Henderson Ranch.

Stagecoach Reservoir lies in a scenic sagebrush basin. A mixture of aspen and lodgepole pine covers the north-facing slopes of the surrounding hills. The most dominant geologic features are the Flattop Mountains to the southwest, the Morrison Mountains to the east, and Blacktail Mountain to the north. The latter peak has unusual volcanic rock formations protruding out from it. Referred to as the Rimrock Outcrop, the vertical stone columns closely resemble those of Devils Tower in northeast Wyoming.

The Colorado Division of Parks and Outdoor Recreation manages the recreational facilities at Stagecoach. The developed areas of this 1,641-acre park are centered along the north shore. The four campgrounds there provide 100 campsites that can accommodate tents, pickup campers, and motor homes. The McKindley Campground near the park entrance is available for walk-in tent camping. Each site has a table and grill, with a vault toilet nearby. The Pinnacle, Harding Spur, and Junction City campgrounds all have tables and grills at each campsite. Additional facilities include flush toilets, water hydrants, and a dump station, with showers located in the camper services building. Junction City is the only campground with electrical hookups at each site.

Day-use facilities include two modern picnic sites. The Haybro picnic area lies north of the marina along the lake. The large Keystone picnic area is west of the Junction City Campground, just south of the park office. Sandwiched between the Junction City and the Pinnacle campgrounds is the Arrowhead group picnic area, which can accommodate up to 100 people. Arrowhead can be reserved in advance by calling the park office.

Stagecoach State Park. Blacktail Mountain and the hills north of the reservoir are considered a wildlife management area.

The Stagecoach Marina offers boat rentals, fuel, a public phone, and fishing and camping accessories. Food and beverages are also available. The boat ramp that serves the lake is located between the two slip docks. The 775-acre, three-mile-long reservoir hosts a variety of water sports. The northeast half of the lake is used for boating, jet skiing, and waterskiing, while the southwest half is reserved for wakeless boating. Directly below the marina concession building is a swim beach. There is no lifeguard on duty, so individuals swim at their own risk. Children under twelve should be accompanied by an adult.

Fishing has become a favorite activity at Stagecoach. Anglers enjoy the abundance of rainbow, cutthroat, and occasionally brown and brook trout. There are several fishing access areas along Routt County Road 18, which parallel the north shoreline and two more at the southwest corner of the lake near the junction of Routt County 14 and Routt County 16. For the energetic angler, or for anyone who desires a scenic hike, a five-mile trail begins at the fishing access area along Routt County 16 and extends along the south shore to the dam. Special regulations apply to fishing in the Yampa River below the dam. It is advisable to check with the park office for current fishing regulations.

Directions:
From Steamboat Springs, drive south 4 miles on U.S. Highway 40. Turn west on Colorado Highway 131 for 5 miles, then turn south on Routt County Road 14 and drive 7 miles to the park entrance. From the junction of Interstate 70 and Colorado 131 at Wolcott, drive north to Phippsburg. About 1.6 miles north of Phippsburg, turn east on Routt County 14 and follow to the park entrance.

Phone or write:
Stagecoach State Park
Box 98
Oak Creek, Colorado 80467
(303) 736-2436

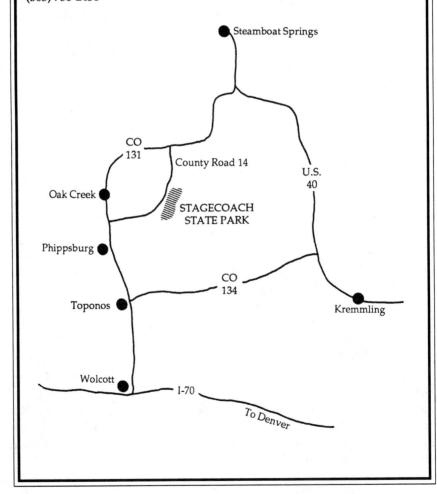

Also at the southwest corner of the park is a seventy-seven-acre wetland habitat reserve designated by the Division of Wildlife. With a pair of binoculars, birdwatchers can observe several species of waterfowl and a variety of other birds, including the great blue heron.

Blacktail Mountain and the hills north of the reservoir are considered a wildlife management area. Special hunting regulations apply in this area, so call the park office for detailed information. The Stagecoach area provides a winter range for elk and is home to a number of other mammals as well. Mule deer, badgers, raccoons, coyotes, ground squirrels, chipmunks and even an occasional black bear are frequently spotted. Public access into this area is restricted from December through March.

During the winter months, the Keystone parking area is plowed and made available for day-use and limited camping. Locals claim that Stagecoach offers the best ice fishing in the state. Cross-country skiing and snowmobiling are other popular activities during the winter season. Snowmobiling is permitted below the high-water line of the reservoir on the frozen surface.

Steamboat Lake State Park

How would you describe a paradise? The word, as defined by *Webster's* dictionary, means a pleasure garden with parks and animal sanctuaries — or a condition of extreme delight.

Welcome to Steamboat Lake State Park (formerly Steamboat Lake State Recreation Area), a paradise in both senses of the word to the 300,000–plus people that visit the park each year. Steamboat Lake lies in the broad basin between the picturesque Hahns Peak to the east and Sand Mountain to the west. Pine-covered hills punctuated with stands of aspen create colorful vistas around an open meadow.

Each season has its own beauty at Steamboat. During the spring the valley floor is carpeted with a sea of wildflowers. The summer months are known for mild temperatures and majestic sunsets. In autumn, as the air turns cool and crisp, the hills become a colorful patchwork of greens, reds, and golds. And during the winter season the earth is blanketed by deep, powdery snow.

The two most visible geographic features in the valley are Hahns Peak and Sand Mountain. Hahns Peak is volcanic in origin and extends 10,839 feet above sea level. The pyramid-shaped mountain was named after German explorer and miner Joseph Hahn, who discovered gold at the base of the peak. George Way named it in honor of his fellow prospector after climbing to the summit on August 27, 1865. Numerous inactive gold and silver mines can still be found on the face of the mountain. The remains of a fire lookout tower built atop the peak by the U.S. Forest Service in 1912 and used until 1946 can be seen clearly from the valley below.

The 10,847-foot Sand Mountain lies to the west of the park. Originally called White Head Peak, it received its present name from the sandy soil found along its eastern slope. The mountain yields a whitish

Steamboat Lake State Park. Several of the original structures of Hahns Peak Village have been renovated and are now part of the Hahns Peak Historical Museum.

quartzite that the Ute Indians used to make stone tools such as scrapes and spear points. The Utes came to the valley every summer and fall to hunt. But the discovery of gold along Hahns Peak during the 1860s brought hundreds of miners and prospectors into the area. As more white settlers entered the valley, the Utes were slowly driven out of their homeland.

With the growth of the mining industry came the formation of Hahns Peak Mining District. Several communities sprang up in the valley with such names as Bugstown, International Camp, and Poverty Flats, whose name was later changed to Hahns Peak Village. For years Hahns Peak Village served as a lively center for miners, ranchers, and homesteaders. It was also the Routt County seat until 1912, and it remains the oldest permanent settlement in Routt County. (Several of the original structures have been renovated and are now part of the Hahns Peak Historical Museum.) As the mining industry came to an end during the 1920s, cattle ranching, logging, and recreation became the major economic base for northern Colorado.

The 2,557-acre park is located in the northern part of Routt County about twenty-six miles north of Steamboat Springs. The dam, built over

Willow Creek, was completed in 1967. Aside from Willow Creek, the 1,053-acre reservoir is fed by Mill Creek, Floyd Creek, Larson Creek, Dutch Creek, and Deep Creek. The main purpose of the lake is to provide a water storage base that is used to cool the generators at the Colorado/Ute Power Plant. But the ingredients that make Steamboat Lake special are scenic beauty, a placid atmosphere, and diverse outdoor activities.

Most of the recreational facilities are located on the north side of the lake. Steamboat has three campgrounds with 183 campsites, most of which are sheltered by a mature lodgepole pine forest. Each campsite can accommodate tents, trailers, pickup campers, and motor homes.

The Sunrise Vista Campground has 103 campsites. All sites are equipped with tables and grills, with water hydrants and vault toilets nearby. At the amphitheater located next to this campground, park rangers and naturalists provide interpretive outdoor programs on Saturday evenings from Memorial Day through Labor Day.

The Dutch Hill and Bridge Island campgrounds are found in the northwest section of the park. Bridge Island can be reached by driving over a canal on a one-lane bridge. Both campgrounds have tables and grills at each site, with vault toilets and water hydrants nearby. Electrical hookups are not available at any of the campgrounds. A dump station is located on the east side of the park along the road that leads to the Sage Flats day-use area.

Just east of the Dutch Hill Campground is the Steamboat Lake Marina, a full-service facility that rents a variety of craft, from paddleboats to pontoon boats. Other services include slip rental, fuel, minor boat repairs, and wet suit rental. This concession also sells groceries and camping and fishing accessories.

Three boat ramps serve the lake — one next to the marina, one at Placer Cove, and one at Sage Flats. Next to the marina there is a swim beach area. No lifeguard monitors the beach, and, at 8,000 feet above sea level, the water is often too cold for safe swimming until mid-June.

Jet skiing, waterskiing, and sailing are other favorite attractions at Steamboat. At the Sage Flats day-use area at the southeast corner of the lake, water-skiers enjoy a designated take-off/drop-off area. A second take-off/drop-off point is located on the southeast shore of Bridge Island. Due to the cold water, water-skiers are advised to wear a full wet suit or dry suit.

Steamboat Lake State Park. The Steamboat Lake Marina is a full-service facility that rents everything from paddleboats to pontoon boats. Other services include slip rental, fuel, minor boat repair, and wet suit rental.

The Placer Cove day-use site, located at the northeast corner of the lake, has numerous picnic tables scattered along the shoreline. At Placer Cove visitors will find the trailhead to the Tombstone Nature Trail. This three-quarter-mile self-guided path has eleven interpretive stations that illustrate the history, wildlife, and vegetation of the park. The Tombstone Nature Trail was named after the James and Rose Wheeler family, who came from Sterling, Colorado, in 1921 in a Model-T to homestead in the valley. Unfortunately, the Wheelers faced difficult times: Two of their children are buried on a forested hill overlooking Placer Cove. The tombstone at interpretive station number 5 marks the gravesite. The Wheeler home has been inundated by the reservoir.

The coves of Steamboat Lake have become famous for their excellent trout fishing. The lake yields over 100,000 fish annually to anglers from across the country. The Colorado Division of Wildlife periodically stocks the lake with rainbow and cutthroat trout. Brook trout often find their way into the lake from the streams that feed it. The two fishing access areas on the west side of the park, Rainbow Ridge and Meadow

225

Directions:
From Steamboat Springs, go west on U.S. Highway 40, turn north on Routt
County Road 129 and drive 26 miles to the park entrance.

Phone or write:
Steamboat Lake State Park
Box 750
Clark, Colorado 80428
(303) 879-3922
Steamboat Lake Marina: (303) 879-7019

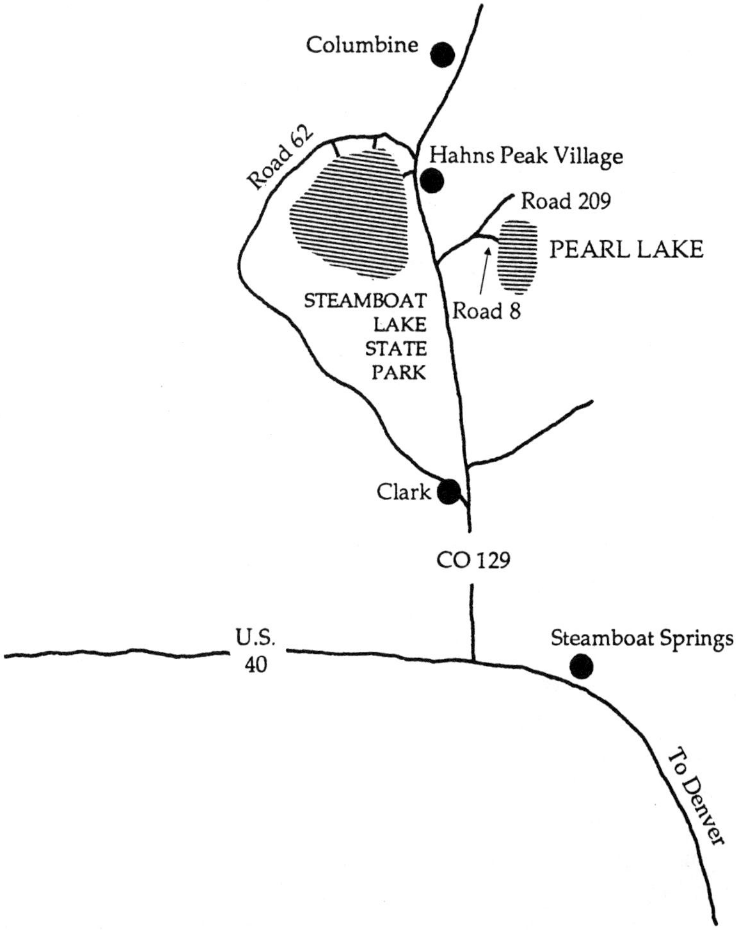

Columbine

Road 62

Hahns Peak Village

Road 209

PEARL LAKE

STEAMBOAT
LAKE
STATE
PARK

Road 8

Clark

CO 129

U.S.
40

Steamboat Springs

To Denver

Point, can be reached by following Routt County Road 62, which begins at the north end of the park.

The hunting of waterfowl, deer, and elk is allowed at Steamboat. However, the use of firearms is prohibited during the summer and controlled during the regular hunting season. The park office has detailed information on the hunting seasons and regulations.

Steamboat Lake is rapidly becoming a winter sports haven. Ice fishing is the biggest winter activity at the park. On any given weekend, the frozen lake is dotted with anglers and their shelters. Snowmobiling is another favorite sport, and the area contains roughly 100 miles of trails to explore. This is one of the few areas in Routt County where snowmobilers are allowed to use county roads. Real adventurers who want to leave the confines of the park can ride seventy miles to Encampment, Wyoming. Cross-country skiers enjoy the man-made trails that meander through the wooded hills surrounding the park.

Aside from scenic beauty, fishing, and water sports, Steamboat Lake State Park provides an ideal setting for nature study and nature photography. At the 8,000-foot altitude, Steamboat Lake falls into the montane life zone. The open valley is characterized by lowland meadows, sagebrush uplands, and knolls covered with stands of pine, aspen, and spruce. Over forty-five species of plants grow vigorously in the rich mountain soil. Blue grass, rabbitbrush, june grass, larkspur, mules-ear, and blue columbine are a few of the many plants that can be seen during the spring and summer seasons.

This diversity of vegetation provides an excellent habitat for a wide variety of wildlife. There have been approximately 200 species of birds sighted in the area, including hawks, eagles, owls, jays, blue grouse, and hummingbirds. The south and west sides of the park are undeveloped and provide a good wetland habitat for waterfowl and shorebirds. Visitors are surprised to learn that the grassy meadows interlaced with willows and marshes create an ideal refuge for the threatened sandhill crane.

The most noticeable mammals in the area are mule deer and elk. Others that populate the region are coyotes, foxes, marmots, black bears, chipmunks, pine squirrels, and ground squirrels.

Sweitzer Lake State Park

Morgan Sweitzer was a man with a vision. A farmer and fruit grower from Delta, Sweitzer dreamed of building a recreation area in the vicinity. In 1953 he donated land to the state with the understanding that it be developed for recreation. Construction began immediately, and additional land was purchased from another farmer, Alex Jennings. Sadly, Morgan Sweitzer did not live to see his dream become a reality — he lost his life in a tractor accident in the summer of 1953.

Sweitzer Lake State Park lies on the arid desertlike terrain of the Western Slope just south of Delta. The lake was built on a large alluvial plain created by sediment from the Gunnison and Uncompahgre rivers. These sediments were eroded and deposited during the uplift of the surrounding mountains. The dam was erected by honor camp inmates of the Colorado State Reformatory. At one time Sweitzer Lake was designated as the work headquarters for the honor camp system. The camp is now set up west of Delta. The lake, part of a loop formed by the Uncompahgre Water Users Irrigation Canal, is filled with water from the canal and wastewater from irrigation ditches.

In 1960 the Colorado Game and Fish Department assumed management of Sweitzer Lake. In 1972 it was transferred again, this time to the Colorado Division of Parks and Outdoor Recreation. This 210-acre park is a day-use area, with picnicking the primary attraction. Families can enjoy several grassy picnic areas in a scenic setting. The snowcapped West Elk Mountains rise to the east, the majestic San Juan Mountains to the south, the Uncompahgre Plateau to the west, and Grand Mesa, the world's largest flattop mountain, to the north.

On hot summer days, the 137-acre lake is a refreshing retreat for visitors. Power boating, sailing, and waterskiing are popular. So is the

Sweitzer Lake State Park. Sweitzer is a 210-acre park that provides family recreation in a scenic setting.

Sweitzer Lake State Park. On hot summer days, Sweitzer Lake is a refreshing retreat for visitors. Boating, waterskiing, and swimming are popular activities.

Directions:
Go 3 miles south of Delta on U.S. Highway 50, then turn east on the park entrance road.

Phone or write:
Sweitzer Lake State Park
1735 E Road
Delta, Colorado 81416
(303) 874-4258

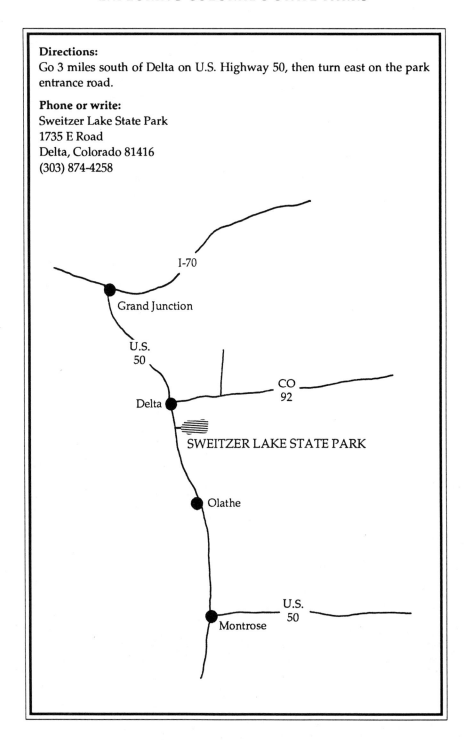

swim beach located on the west side of the lake. No lifeguard is on duty, so swimmers do so at their own risk.

Sweitzer Lake has a good reputation among fishermen for carp, catfish, and bluegill. However, anglers are advised not to eat the fish they catch. In 1958 wildlife biologists discovered high levels of selenium in the fish. (Selenium is a chemical element of the sulfur group that occurs naturally in the shale beneath the lake.) It is uncertain how many fish people can consume before the chemical affects them. The shore along the lake's west side, near the boat ramp, has been adapted to provide a safe area for handicapped fishermen.

Nature lovers observe and photograph mule deer, rabbits, raccoons, and pheasants at Sweitzer. The Audobon Society has named Sweitzer as a bird-watching and waterfowl observation area. Approximately 179 species of birds have been sighted in this area, white pelicans, egrets, cormorants, and great blue herons among them.

Hunting is restricted to waterfowl during the regular hunting season, usually October through January. Hunters can take advantage of the five blinds along the south shore and three blinds along the north and east sides.

Sylvan Lake State Park

Located only sixteen miles south of Eagle along West Brush Creek Road, Sylvan Lake State Park is one of Colorado's best-kept secrets, a scenic getaway for people who enjoy peace and quiet. The park sits in the middle of White River National Forest. Visitors enjoy a 360-degree panoramic view of majestic mountain scenery. Many people favor visiting Sylvan in September to celebrate the turning of the aspen. As the days grow shorter and cooler temperatures prevail, the pale green aspen leaves turn bright yellow, creating patches of gold in the conifer forest. The vivid yellow and green hues against the red sandstone cliffs create an unforgettable scene.

This 155-acre park was originally a mink farm owned by Otto Zurcher. In the 1940s Zurcher built the dam across Brush Creek that created Sylvan Lake, which at that time was called the O.Z. Reservoir. Because of tax problems, Zurcher lost the property in 1963. For the next several years, the land was open to the public for fishing and camping. In 1973 it became the Sylvan Lake State Fishing Area, managed by the Division of Wildlife. On July 1, 1987, the land was traded to the Division of Parks and Outdoor Recreation for another section of land. From that point forward, it has been called Sylvan Lake State Park.

Aside from natural beauty, fishing is Sylvan's main attraction. This forty-acre lake is an angler's paradise, heavily stocked with rainbow and brook trout by the Colorado Division of Wildlife. In fact, it is one of the few lakes in Colorado stocked with brook trout. Boats with electric motors and nonmotorized boats, such as rubber rafts or canoes, are the only craft allowed on the lake. Ice fishing is available in winter, along with the popular sports of cross-country skiing and snowmobiling.

Careful observers can find wildlife such as mule deer, cottontail rabbits, and chipmunks taking refuge in the clusters of willows that

SYLVAN LAKE STATE PARK

Directions:
From the Eagle exit on Interstate 70, drive south through Eagle on Main Street. Turn right and drive south on Brush Creek Road, which becomes West Brush Creek Road. The park entrance is 16 miles south of Eagle.

Phone or Write:
Sylvan Lake State Park
c/o Rifle Gap State Park
0050 Road 219
Rifle, Colorado 81650
(303) 625-1607

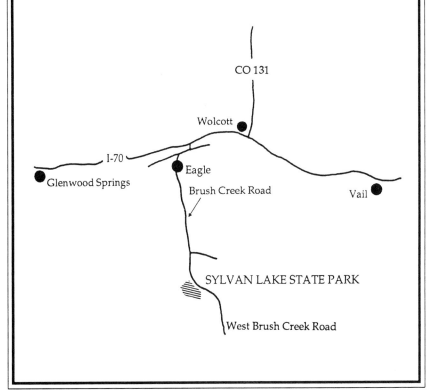

Sylvan Lake State Park. Aside from the natural beauty of the area, fishing is the main attraction. The lake is heavily stocked with rainbow and brook trout by the Colorado Division of Wildlife. In fact, Sylvan is one of the few lakes in Colorado where brook trout are stocked.

grow along Brush Creek. The fishing access trail that circles the lake brings hikers close to several species of waterfowl feeding along the shore.

Sylvan has two campgrounds that provide fifty campsites — thirty at Elk Run and twenty at Fisherman's Paradise. Both campgrounds can accommodate tents, trailers, campers, and motor homes. Each site is equipped with a table and grill as well as flush toilets and chemical toilets nearby.

Trinidad Lake State Park

When it comes to history, the area surrounding Trinidad Lake State Park is one of the richest in Colorado. It seems as though every stream, road, mountain, and building here has its own legend. The history of the Trinidad region and the Purgatoire Valley can be divided into two time periods. In the first era, prior to 1900, Spanish-American people explored and settled the area. After 1900 the railroad extended into the valley and coal mining became the dominant industry.

By studying artifacts from several sites in and around the park area, archaeologists have determined that life in the region dates back to the early Sopris Phase (A.D. 1075 through A.D. 1150). The most widespread Native American tribes were the Jicarilla Apache, Utes, and Comanches.

Precise records of the early Spanish expeditions into southern Colorado are sketchy. Historians believe that Don Juan Onate and his men may have been the first Spanish explorers to enter Colorado, coming via the San Luis Valley in 1598. That would be approximately twenty-two years before the Pilgrims landed at Plymouth Rock. The first documented expedition into the Purgatoire Valley was led by Juan Archuleta in 1664. Archuleta's mission was to retrieve runaway Indians from Taos Pueblo. These Indians staged an unsuccessful rebellion and sought refuge with the Apaches in El Cuartilego along the Arkansas River. In 1706 Juan de Ulibarri led another expedition into Colorado through the mouth of Long's Canyon, which is within the present-day park boundaries.

Don Antonio Valverde Cosio ventured into what is now Colorado in 1719. Valverde, the governor of the Spanish territory of New Mexico, had two objectives in mind: He wanted to punish the Comanches, who were harassing Spanish settlers, and to investigate rumors about the

French intruding into Spanish territory. Valverde is credited with renaming the Purgatoire River as he marched across the plains. Originally known as El Rio de las Animas Perdidas en Purgatorio, "The River of Lost Souls in Purgatory," Valverde changed the name to Las Animas, a name that lasted roughly seventy years. According to legend (and there are several versions to the story), the river is named in honor of Antonio Gutierrez Humana. Humana and Francisco Leyba de Bonilla led a gold-hunting expedition along the river as it flowed across the plains. They had orders to return to headquarters if no gold was found. Leyba and a small group of men were ready to return, but Humana wanted to continue. A quarrel between the leaders separated the expedition. Leyba and his men turned back, while Humana and a small group of hopefuls pushed on. The priest who was traveling with the gold seekers went with the group that returned to headquarters. Years later the skeletal remains and armor of the Humana's group were found along the river bank. Apparently they were ambushed by angry Indians. With no priest accompanying them, these poor men died without the benefit of last rites — hence, they were the lost souls in purgatory.

In later years the French fur trappers shortened the name to La Purgatoire. Mountain men and Anglo settlers mispronounced and misspelled the name until it became "Picketwire." Today we use the French spelling Purgatoire, but pronounce it "purgatory."

The city of Trinidad (which means "Trinity" in Spanish) has a turbulent and flamboyant past of its own. It was a home and resting place for many famous people: town marshall and saloon owner Bat Masterson, U.S. Marshall and stagecoach driver Wyatt Earp, frontier scout Kit Carson, who often passed through the area, and notorius outlaw Billy the Kid.

In 1876 coal mines began operating in the Upper Purgatoire Valley. By the turn of the century, coal mining had replaced farming and ranching as the major industry; by 1930 there were over fifty coal mining companies in the valley. After World War II, the demand for coal decreased, and the coal mining industry rapidly declined by 1950. Only two mines are in operation today. The area has made a gradual economic recovery. With the abundance of historical sites, museums, and recreation opportunities, tourism is slowly becoming the dominant resource in the Purgatoire Valley.

Located only three miles west of Trinidad, Trinidad Lake was built by the U.S. Army Corps of Engineers as a multipurpose project for flood control, irrigation, and recreation. The dam over the Purgatoire River was authorized by the Flood Control Act of 1958. Construction began in the early 1970s and was completed in 1978. The recreational facilities were opened to the public in 1981 under the management of the Colorado Division of Parks and Outdoor Recreation.

About 1,500 residents from the communities of Carpios, Sopris, Piedmont, Jerryville, St. Thomas, Sopris Plaza, and Viola had to be relocated prior to construction of the dam. Even the Carpios cemetery was moved. These towns were located along the south side of today's Trinidad Lake. The only visible signs of the former communities are the slag piles of the Sopris Mine and the rock insignia "LHS," for Lincoln High School, which served the area.

Upon government acquisition of the land, the anthropology department of Trinidad State Junior College, under contract with the National Park Service, salvaged as many archaeological artifacts as possible. Forty-eight sites were found within the present-day park boundaries. All cultural recoveries found at these sites were identified and curated by 1980 in accordance with all federal laws and orders for the preservation of historic and prehistoric remains. Detailed notes of the operation are contained in the Trinidad Lake Cultural Resource Study. Parts one and two of the study are on file at the park office. Most of the artifacts found are now on display at the Army Corps of Engineers Information Center.

Trinidad is now a 2,300-acre park that provides unlimited outdoor recreation. Carpios Ridge along the north side is the most developed section of the park. Visitors will find picnic facilities and an ultramodern campground. The picnic loop features two group picnic shelters that can accommodate fifty people. Both shelters can be reserved in advance. There are twenty-eight single picnic sites available with tables and grills. Facilities include restrooms with flush toilets, drinking fountains, horseshoe pits, and a children's playground.

Near the center of the picnic grounds is the Indian Teepee interpretive site, one of the archaeological sites discovered by the Trinidad State Junior College anthropology department. Arapahoe or Ute Indians probably camped on this hill during the eighteenth century. The stones were used to secure the teepees at their circular base, hence the name "teepee rings."

At the Carpios Ridge Overlook, visitors will find a scenic view of the lake and Fisher's Peak. With an elevation of 9,655 feet, Fisher's Peak

Trinidad Lake State Park. Near the center of the picnic grounds is the Indian Teepee interpretive site. This site was probably used by the Arapahoe or Ute Indians who camped on this hill during the eighteenth century. The stones were used to secure the teepees at their circular base, hence the name "teepee rings."

is the most prominent landmark in the area. Several legends purport to explain how the peak got its name. The most accepted is that on August 6, 1846, Captain Waldemar Fisher of the U.S. Army climbed the peak. The captain's alleged venture was part of the invasion of the West by Colonel Stephen Watts Kearney's army, which marched from Bent's Fort into the Republic of Mexico during the Mexican-American War.

A plaque was placed at the overlook on May 16, 1981, by the board of county commissioners, in honor of the many residents who lived in the area and the many persons who made the dam a reality. From the overlook, visitors can clearly view the south side of the valley, the slag piles from the Sopris Mine, and the "LHS" rock insignia of the defunct Lincoln High School.

Trinidad Lake's campground features three loops with sixty-two campsites for tents, trailers, and large motor homes. Thirty-one sites are set up with tent pads, forty-nine have electrical hookups, and five are designed for handicapped persons. Each campsite is equipped with a table and grill. Facilities include restrooms with flush toilets, showers, a

Trinidad Lake State Park. At the Carpios Ridge Overlook, visitors will find a scenic view of the lake and Fisher's Peak.

laundry room, water hydrants, and a dump station. For entertainment, there are several horseshoe pits, a playground, and group fire rings. An amphitheater lies between the campground and the picnic area. Campfire programs are presented here by park rangers on weekends and holidays, Memorial Day through Labor Day.

An entrance next to the Army Corps of Engineers information center in the northeast corner of the park leads to the only boat ramp that serves the lake. This area has ample space for boat trailers, along with several picnic sites. The road continues across the dam before reaching the south side entrance road. From here, motorists have a spectacular view of the lake and the Culebra Range of the Sangre de Cristo Mountains to the west. To the east, Fisher's Peak towers over the communities of Jansen and Trinidad. (Stopping and parking on the dam are prohibited.) The south side entrance road serves as a major fishing access route. The only facilities are six sheltered picnic sites and several chemical toilets.

The west side of the lake can be reached by going south on the Reilly Canyon access road off Colorado Highway 12 to the northwest shore. At the junction of the Reilly Canyon road and Colorado 12 are the

Trinidad Lake State Park. On the southwest side of the junction of Colorado Highway 12 and Reilly Canyon Road are the remains of the Cokedale Ovens. These were used around the turn of the century to produce coke, a by-product of coal used in the manufacturing of steel.

remains of the Cokedale Ovens. These ovens were used around the turn of the century to produce "coke," a byproduct of coal used in the manufacturing of steel.

Another interesting set of remains are in Long's Canyon. Long's Canyon can be reached by following Las Animas County Road 18.3, which extends south from Colorado 12 just east of Madrid. Once into the canyon, visitors will find an abandoned Penitente religious site. The ruins consist of several adobe buildings, a wooden church, and a cemetery. This site is on private property and is posted against trespassing. However, the buildings can be viewed from the road. Like many remote Hispanic settlements in southern Colorado and northern New Mexico, this abandoned village had strong ties with *Los Hermanos de Luz* (The Brothers of Light), commonly called Penitentes. These religious brotherhoods were lay organizations that had their roots in the Catholic Church, but they were looked upon with disapproval by the church hierarchy. They were best known for their dramatic and often secret rites during Easter week dramatizing Christ's passion.

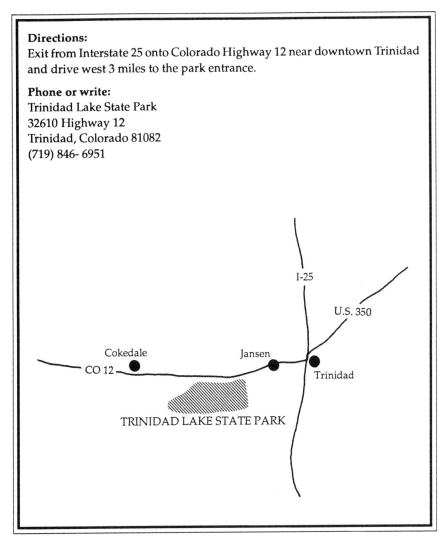

Directions:
Exit from Interstate 25 onto Colorado Highway 12 near downtown Trinidad and drive west 3 miles to the park entrance.

Phone or write:
Trinidad Lake State Park
32610 Highway 12
Trinidad, Colorado 81082
(719) 846- 6951

For those who seek to explore the backcountry, there are several hiking trails. Two begin in the campground, just west of the shower house. The three-quarter-mile Carpios Ridge Trail is a steep, scenic route that extends along the north shoreline to the picnic area. The Levsa Canyon Loop Trail, a 1.5-mile self-guided nature trail, circles through the dense piñon pine and junipers that are common in southern Colorado. Fifteen stations illustrate the plants and historical sites along the trail. The Reilly Canyon Trail, an extension of the Levsa Canyon Trail, continues 5.0 miles (one way) into Reilly Canyon on the west side of the park near the historic town of Cokedale. The Carpios Cove Trail begins near the group picnic sites and follows the shore for three-fourths of a mile, providing fishing access. On the south side of the park along the access road, visitors will find the South Shore Trailhead. This 2.0-mile trail (one way) extends through a wildlife area on the southwest side of the park before entering Long's Canyon.

Water sports at Trinidad Lake include sailing, waterskiing, and jet skiing. Swimming is prohibited. Boaters are warned to be alert to submerged hazards. As the water level decreases, land outcroppings will appear west of the boat ramp and along the south shore. Fishing is permitted anywhere on the lake with the exception of the boat launching area. The reservoir is periodically stocked with rainbow and brown trout, bass, catfish, walleye, crappie, and bluegill.

Small game hunting is allowed in designated areas during the regular hunting season. Only shotguns and bows and arrows are permitted.

Vega State Park

People who thrive on tranquility and enjoy great fishing, can find both at Vega State Park (formerly Vega State Recreation Area). *Vega* is a Spanish word meaning "meadow," and the name is justified, as the park lies in an open area called "the meadows" at the eastern edge of the Plateau Valley. This placid valley is surrounded on three sides — as if by a giant horseshoe — by Grand Mesa National Forest. The park itself is sandwiched between two geological landmarks, Battlement Mesa to the north and Grand Mesa, the world's largest flattop mountain, to the south.

Located approximately fifty-seven miles east of Grand Junction, this high mountain valley at 8,000 feet was once covered by the sea. Back in the Paleozoic Era, roughly 250 million to 500 million years ago, the opposing forces of uplift and erosion had already begun sculpting Grand Mesa and the surrounding landscape. The most interesting event during that era was the advancement and recession of the oceans. As the sea receded, it left layers of sedimentary sandstone, shale, and limestone. Between 70 million and 250 million years ago, the area was transformed into a tropical swamp. Evidence of ancient animal life remains in the form of fossilized tortoise shells found throughout the valley.

Records show that the first Europeans to enter the Plateau Valley were the ten members of the famous Dominguez-Escalante Expedition of 1776. Their goal was to establish a route from Santa Fe, New Mexico, to Monterey, California, which was the Spanish cultural center of the Pacific Coast. The first settlers in the meadows were the members of the Hawxhurst family during the fall of 1881. It is believed that they entered the valley by traveling the same basic route used by the Dominguez-Escalante Expedition 105 years earlier. They survived the long, cold

Vega State Park. First-time visitors to the Plateau Valley are amazed to see cattle being driven through the streets of Collbran and along Colorado Highway 330. Before reaching the high mountain meadows, the cattle are driven across the Vega Dam on the west side of the park.

winter before moving to the lower valley near present-day Collbran in the spring of 1882.

From 1881 through 1900 the meadows area was used as a cattle-holding area for ranchers in the valley. During this time, early pioneers built the small town of Vega at a site now inundated by the Vega Reservoir. By 1891 Vega had a general store, two sawmills, a school, a church, a cemetery, and a post office. The latter was used until 1914, when it was transferred to Collbran, twelve miles to the west. Roughly 100 people, including twelve families, lived in and around Vega.

In 1959 the U.S. Bureau of Reclamation, in cooperation with the Collbran Water Conservancy District, began building the Vega Dam over Plateau Creek, just west of the town of Vega. Completed in 1962, the 896-acre reservoir provides irrigation for farmers and ranchers in the Plateau Valley. Aside from Plateau Creek, the lake is fed by the Leon Creek Feeder Canal, Leon Creek, and Park Creek.

Prior to construction of the dam, the main house from the old Campbell Ranch was moved north, just outside the park boundary. It has been refurbished and is now known as the Vega Lodge. This commercial establishment provides food, lodging, fuel, and boating and fishing accessories to local residents and park visitors. Unfortunately, the rest of the historic structures lie beneath the lake. Even the Vega cemetery is submerged. In cooperation with the descendents of those buried there, a monument was placed along the east shore of the island area to honor these early pioneers. The actual location of the cemetery is roughly 220 feet east of the marker. The inundated town of Vega is south of the island area at the lake's north end.

First-time visitors to the Plateau Valley are amazed to see cattle being driven through the streets of Collbran and along Colorado Highway 330. During the late spring and early summer, ranchers drive their cattle from the lower valley to the summer grazing pastures in the alpine meadows. When the herds reach Vega State Park, they are driven across the dam to an area south of the reservoir. The cattle are returned to the lower elevations in late autumn, prior to the big-game hunting season and preferably before the season's first snowstorm.

There are four major ecosystems found in and around the park. One of them, the marshland along the east shore, is a result of the man-made lake. The shrub community provides an abundance of scrub oak along the east and south shorelines, while the sagebrush community is found throughout the park. Dense aspen groves cover the hillside along the south shore. The most diverse plant community occupies the riparian zone that follows Plateau Creek.

In late spring and early summer, the meadow becomes a sea of wildflowers. A colorful array of mules-ears, Indian paintbrush, and a variety of other flowers add a splash of color to the lush green valley. Blue columbines are found swinging with the gentle breeze along the south shore and throughout the aspen forest.

With the completion of the reservoir, the meadows changed from an agricultural area to a recreational area. The 1,830-acre park, a year-round paradise for outdoor enthusiasts, is managed by the Colorado Division of Parks and Outdoor Recreation.

There are four campgrounds that provide 109 campsites for tents, trailers, and large motor homes. Each campsite is equipped with a table and grill. Electrical hookups are not available at Vega.

The Vega Cove Campground, with twenty-one campsites, is located on a small island connected to the north shore by a man-made dirt road. Near the center of the island is a picnic area with a playground. Vault toilets and water hydrants are available for the camping and picnic areas. The island provides two of the three boat ramps that serve the lake. One ramp is used when the water level is high, the other when the water is low due to irrigation.

The Oak Point Campground is also found on the north side of the lake. Most of the forty campsites are located along the shoreline. Oak Point has one flush toilet, along with several vault toilets scattered throughout the campground. Other facilities include water hydrants, a dump station, and the third boat ramp along the west side.

The Aspen Grove Campground is located in the southeast corner of the park. These forty sites are nestled in seclusion between clumps of willows. Aspen Grove also provides a group camping area with tables, grills, water hydrants, and vault toilets. Next to the campground is the Meadows group picnic shelter, which can accommodate up to thirty people. Adjacent to the picnic area is an open field for games such as softball and volleyball.

The fourth campground, Marmot Flats, is on the west side of the park just south of the dam. This group camping site is considered rustic; vault toilets are available, but drinking water is not.

Day-use facilities include the Turtle Shell picnic area located on the northeast corner of the lake. There are numerous picnic sites scattered around the shoreline. Swimming is prohibited at Vega; at 8,000 feet above sea level, the water is usually too cold for safe swimming. Waterskiing is popular from early June through mid-August. However, skiers are advised to wear wet suits or dry suits.

At the southwest corner of the park, visitors will find the Vega Nature Trail. This 1.25-mile trail has four interpretive stations that illustrate the wildlife, plantlife, and geology of the area. The trail meanders through the dense aspen forest before crossing the road and continuing along the south shore. Park rangers often lead interpretive walks for schools and youth groups. Appointments can be made in advance.

Vega is home to a variety of wildlife. Elk, beaver, rabbits, and waterfowl thrive in the lush valley. It's not unusual to see mule deer feeding near the campgrounds or to hear coyotes yelping during the night.

Near the Vega Nature Trail is the beginning of the Leon Creek Road. This is a four-wheel-drive and dirt-bike road that extends approximately twenty-four miles onto the Grand Mesa before connecting with Colorado Highway 65.

Directions:
From Interstate 70, go east on Colorado Highway 65 for 10 miles, then east on Colorado Highway 330 through Collbran for 12 miles to the park entrance.

Phone or write:
Vega State Park
Box 186
Collbran, Colorado 81624
(303) 487-3407

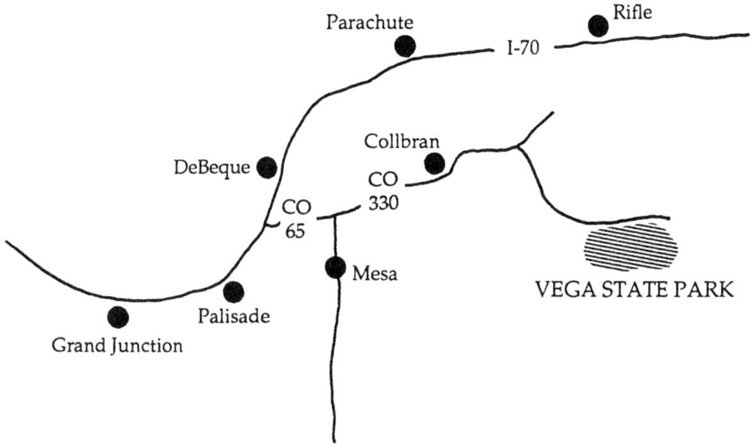

Rifle
Parachute
I-70
Collbran
DeBeque
CO
CO 330
65
Mesa
Palisade
VEGA STATE PARK
Grand Junction

Hunting is not allowed within the park boundaries. However, Vega is often used as a base camp for big-game hunters during the regular hunting season.

The clean, clear water of Vega provides some of the best trout fishing in Colorado. Record-sized rainbow and cutthroat trout are common here. Cold-weather enthusiasts can take advantage of the great ice fishing offered at Vega. However, the big winter attraction is snowmobiling. Between Vega and the adjacent Grand Mesa, there are eight marked trails that provide roughly 170 miles of scenic trails. The area gets an average snowfall of four to six feet anually.

Passes, Permits, and Reservations

Passes and Permits:

Visitors to all Colorado state parks are required to display a current Colorado State Parks Pass on their auto windshield. There are two types of passes: a day pass, which is valid from the day of purchase until noon the following day, and an annual pass, which is valid at any Colorado state park for the remainder of the calendar year. For annual pass holders who own a second car, a second pass is available for a reduced fee. Passes can be purchased at self-service dispensers at any park entrance, or at any park headquarters. Prices are subject to change.

In addition to a parks pass, campers are required to purchase and display a camping permit at their campsite. Permits are good from the day of purchase until noon the following day.

Colorado residents sixty-two years of age or older qualify for a special Aspen Leaf Annual Pass, available at a discounted rate. These allow admission to all state parks every day and free camping on weekdays. A camping fee is charged on weekends and holidays. A fee is also charged for electric hookups, where available.

Those displaying Colorado Disabled Veteran (DV) license plates are admitted free without a pass.

Cherry Creek, Eldorado, and Arkansas Headwaters require a separate, additional day pass, which is discussed in the individual chapters.

Each year the Colorado Division of Parks and Outdoor Recreation publishes a detailed list of the most current park regulations, including those covering hunting and fishing, boat registration, and backcountry use. This brochure also lists a variety of safety tips and is free at any park entrance or park headquarters.

Reservations:

Camping reservations may be made ten to sixty days in advance. Each campsite may be reserved for up to two weeks at a time. To make reservations, call:

Denver Metro area — 470-1144
Outside of Denver area — (800) 678-2267

Group campgrounds, group picnic areas, and other day-use facilities can be reserved by calling the individual park headquarters.

Main Office
1313 Sherman St., #618
Denver, Colorado 80203
(303) 866-3437

North Region
3842 S. Mason, #8
Fort Collins, Colorado 80525
(303) 226-6641

South Region
2126 N. Weber
Colorado Springs, Colorado 80907
(719) 471-0900

West Region
222 S. 6th., #420-B
Grand Junction, Colorado 81501
(303) 248-7319

Metro Region
13787 S. Highway 85
Littleton, Colorado 80125
(303) 791-1957

Index

Pages set in bold type indicate references to maps. Pages set in italic type refer to captions of illustrations.

Denver and Hudson Canal, 23, 25
Denver Land and Water Storage Company, 37
Denver R/C Eagles Club, 53, *54*
Denver Reservoir and Irrigation Company, 21
Denver and Rio Grande Railroad, 5, 191
Denver and Rio Grande Western Railroad, 171
Desert terrain: of Cactus Valley and Silt Mesa region, 89; of Western Slope, 94, 228
Diamond Peaks, 59
Dinosaur Hill, 96
Divide, **169**
Dixon Grove, Cherry Creek, 51, 54
Dodge Expedition (1835), 188
Dog training, 46, 53–54
Dome Rock, *150*, 170
Dome Rock Natural Area, 166, 170
Dome Rock Trail, Mueller Park, 168, 170
Dome Rock Wildlife Area, Mueller Park, 166, 168
Dominguez-Escalante Expedition (1776), 243
Dutch Charlie recreation site, Ridgway Park, 192–194, 197
Dutch Creek, 224
Dutch Hill Campground, Steamboat Lake Park, 224

E

Eagle, 232, 233
Eagle picnic area, Rifle Gap Park, 206
Eagles: bald, 18–20, *19*, 94, 100; golden, 95, 125
Eagle Trail, Golden Gate Canyon, 85
Earp, Wyatt, 236
Earth Day 1990 tree planting, 53
Earthquake (1923), 66
East Beach Campground, Bonny Park, 28
East Rifle Creek, 91, *155*, 198, 201
East Sand Hills, 62
Ecosystems, variety of in one park, 208, 210, 245. *See also* Forest ecosystem; Mountain ecosystem; Prairie
Ecotone, 122

Edna Mine, 217
Egrets, 18, 95, 231
Eisenhower, Dwight and Mamie, 72
El Cuartilego, 235
Eldorado Canyon State Park, 71–75, *72*, *73*, *141*, 249
Eldorado Canyon Trail, 74
Eldorado Hotel, 72
Eldorado Springs, 72, 73
Eleven Mile Canyon, 76, 213
Eleven Mile Dam, 76–77, 79
Eleven Mile Reservoir, *142*
Eleven Mile State Park, 76–79, *77*, *78*, **79**, *142*, 213
Eleven Mile State Recreation Area, 1
Elk Ridge Campground, Ridgway Park, 193, 194
Elk Run Campground, Sylvan Lake Park, 234
Elk Trail, Golden Gate Canyon, 85–86
Eltuck Bay, Lory Park, 126
Eltuck group picnic area, Lory Park, 125, 126
Encampment, Wyoming, snowmobiling to, 227
Epeneter, Gus and Ruth, 99
Equestrian cross-country jumping, 125, *148*
Escalante, Silvestre Velez de, 129

F

Fairplay, 76
Falls Trail, Castlewood Canyon Park, 40
Farmers Irrigation Company, 91, 92
Farmers Reservoir and Irrigation Company, 21
Farming. *See* Agriculture
Farwell Mountain, 183
FIBArk (First in Boating on the Arkansas), 9
Fisher, Waldemar, 238
Fisherman's Bridge, Arkansas Headwaters, 8
Fisherman's Paradise Campground, Sylvan Lake Park, 234
Fisher's Peak, 237–238, 239
Fishing: access areas, 10, 70, 119, 206, 225,

INDEX

I

access to, 45, 51, 190, 194; modern facilities for, 34; prohibited, 131, 216,
242, 246; warm-water, 68–69, 96–97
Sylvan Lake State Park, *162*, 232–234, **233**,
234

T

Tallgrass prairie, 26–27, 29–30
Teal picnic area, Rifle Gap Park, 206
Teller City, 58, 59
Telluride, 191, 192
Tents, yurts on trails, 65. *See under*
Campgrounds
Tertiary Period, formation of Rockies,
208, 210
Thirty-nine-mile Mountain, 213
Thorodin Mountain, 85
Thunder Pass, backcountry trail to, 60
Timber industry, 58, 80, 223
Timber Trail, Lory Park, 126
Timber Trail group picnic area, Lory
Park, 125, 126
Toll road (1859), Golden Gate Canyon, 80
Tombstone Nature Trail, Steamboat Lake
Park, 225
Tower Loop fishing area, Cherry Creek,
51
Trails of Golden Gate Canyon, 88
Transfer Campground, Mancos Park, 132
Tremont Mountain, 81, 86
Trinidad, 236, 239, **241**
Trinidad Lake, 236–237
Trinidad Lake Cultural Resource Study,
237
Trinidad Lake State Park, *163*, 235–242,
238, 239, 240, **241**
Trinidad State Junior College, 237
Trout, improvement of habitat, 10. *See
also* Fishing, trout
Turkey vultures, 30, 42
Turquoise Lake, 109
Turtle Shell picnic area, Vega Park, 246
Twelve Mile House, 51
Twelve Mile picnic area, Cherry Creek, 56
Twin Creek Loop campground, Golden
Gate Canyon Park, 83–84

Twin Lakes, 109

U

U.S. Army Corps of Engineers, 1, 44, 237;
dam construction, 44, 51, 236–237
U.S. Bureau of Indian Affairs, 172
U.S. Bureau of Land Management, 6
U.S. Bureau of Reclamation: dam con-
struction, 27, 66, 130, 172, 178, 190,
203, 244; Fryingpan-Arkansas Project,
108; Navajo Irrigation Project, 172; rec-
reation facilities, 109, 192
U.S. Cavalry, forcible removal of Utes, 70
U.S. Department of the Interior, 207
U.S. Fish and Wildlife Service, 94
U.S. Forest Service, 58, 222
Ulibarri, Juan de, 4, 235
Uncompahgre Plateau, 190, 228
Uncompahgre River, 190, 195, 228
Uncompahgre Valley, history of, 190–191
Uncompahgre Water Users Irrigation Ca-
nal, 228
Union Colony, 59
Uphoff, Dave, 30
Upper Arkansas Canyon. *See* Bighorn
Sheep Canyon
Upper Yampa Valley, 217
Upper Yampa Water Conservancy Dis-
trict, 217
User fees, 2
Ute Indians, 72, 117, 171, 182, 217, 223,
235; campsites of, 99, 237; dominance
of mountains, 57, 76, 80, 213; forced re-
moval of, 70, 89; hunting grounds of,
99, 165, 182
Ute Pass, trails to, 63
Ute Pass–Muddy Park Zone, 62

V

Vallie Bridge Recreation Site, Arkansas
Headwaters, 9
Valverde Cosio, Don Antonio, 235–236
Vega, 244–245
Vega cemetery, 245

INDEX

X

Xerces Society, 124

Y

Yale, Mount, 7
Yampa River, 217, 219
Yellow Jacket Pass, 218
Young, Jean, 95
Young Adult Conservation Corps, 16, 130

Yucca Campground, Lathrop Park, 121
Yucca Flats Campground, Lake Pueblo
    Park, 111–112
Yurts on trails, 65

Z

Zerbe, Allen, 201
Zimmerman, John, 59
Zurcher, Otto, 232